# Daily

GRADE
6

# Word Problems
## Math

**The following illustrations were created by the artists listed (provided through Shutterstock.com) and are protected by copyright:** Julianka, Klara Viskova, lilac (page 7); Curly Roo, MatiasDelCarmine (pages 11–13); forden (page 13); Alexander_P (pages 14–16); JelenaA (pages 17–19); Lorelyn Medina (pages 20–25); E.Druzhinina, freesoulproduction (page 22); Sondel Design (pages 29–31); SlipFloat (pages 32–34, 55); Yayayoyo (pages 35–37, 85, 116–118); Alex_Bond, Kate Kalita (page 37); CloudyStock (pages 38–40); HelenField (page 40); bazzier (pages 44–46); bfGrafik (pages 50–52); MarijaPiliponyte (page 52); ONYXprj (pages 53–55); Sunflowerr (pages 56–58); NB_Factory (pages 62–64); Fire_Irbis (pages 65–67); GraphicsRF (pages 67, 106); Svetlana Prikhnenko (pages 68–70); AVS-Images (page 70); HitToon, Olesia Bulycheva (pages 71–73); Nicoleta Ionescu (pages 77–79); olllikeballoon (pages 80–82); Irbena (pages 83–85); nikiteev_konstantin (page 85); avtor painter, Zvereva Iana (page 88); JSlavy (pages 89–91); Pushkin (page 100); Panda Vector (pages 101–103); Arthur Shlain (page 103); durantelallera, James Steidl, Stokkete (page 106); Gossip (pages 107–109); yuriytsirkunov (page 109); Jason Stitt (pages 113–115); Drawn To Be Wild (page 118)

Writing: Vicky Shiotsu
Content Editing: Kathleen Jorgensen
Copy Editing: Cathy Harber
Art Direction: Yuki Meyer
Cover Design: Yuki Meyer
Illustration: Bryan Langdo
Design/Production: Jessica Onken

EMC 3096

**Evan-Moor**®
*Helping Children Learn*

Visit
*teaching-standards.com*
to view a correlation
of this book.
This is a free service.

**Correlated to
Current Standards**

**Congratulations on your purchase of some of the
finest teaching materials in the world.**

*Photocopying the pages in this book
is permitted for <u>single-classroom use only</u>.
Making photocopies for additional classes
or schools is prohibited.*

For information about other Evan-Moor products, call 1-800-777-4362,
fax 1-800-777-4332, or visit our website, www.evan-moor.com.
Entire contents © 2019 EVAN-MOOR CORP.
18 Lower Ragsdale Drive, Monterey, CA 93940-5746. Printed in USA.

CPSIA: Printed by McNaughton & Gunn, Saline, MI USA. [1/2019]

# CONTENTS

# What's New in *Daily Word Problems*

This 10- to 15-minute daily warm-up has been revised and updated to support 21st-century math skills.

## The updated activities provide the following:

- practice with multiple-step problems
- increased opportunities to explain thinking
- understanding of math concepts, number relationships, and operations
- application of math concepts and operations
- a more rigorous student contribution

## *Daily Word Problems* still provides the following:

- short, easy-to-read word problems that students can complete independently
- a progression from basic to more challenging problems and skills
- practice of grade-level skills and review of previously learned skills
- engaging child-friendly weekly themes

## Getting the most out of *Daily Word Problems*

Try these strategies for extending the *Daily Word Problems* warm-up and incorporating it into your regular math lesson:

- Encourage students to diagram or model the situation in the problem. Provide students with scratch paper if needed.

- Encourage students to ask themselves if their answer makes sense and to check their answer using a different method.

- Invite students to identify patterns, explain concepts, or compare strategies with a partner or in small groups.

- Include discussions as a regular part of your math lessons. Encourage discussion of the situation in the problem, mathematical reasoning, and multiple strategies and approaches to solving the problem.

Daily Word Problems • EMC 3096 • © Evan-Moor Corp.

# What's in *Daily Word Problems*

## 36 Theme-Based Weekly Units

### Days 1 through 4

Half-page word problems offer practice using a variety of grade-level or review skills. Work space is included.

### Day 5

A full-page activity provides more rigor and often features a chart, graph, map, or other graphic display, a multiple-step problem, or several problems for students to complete.

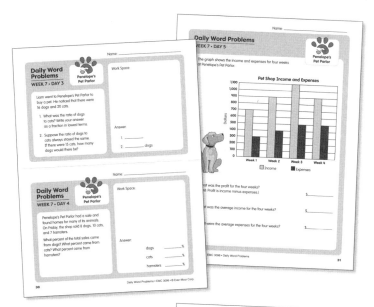

## Additional Features

### Scope and Sequence

The chart on pages 8 and 9 shows the skills practiced each week.

### *My Progress* Chart

Students can monitor their own progress by recording and analyzing their weekly scores. The blackline master for the chart is on page 10.

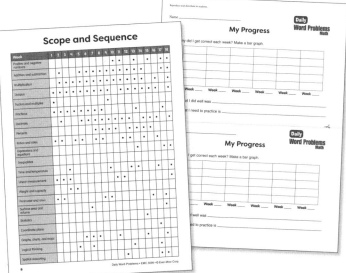

### Answer Key

The answer key provides the answer for each day's problem. If a problem is open-ended, a description of the type of valid answer is given. Accept any reasonable response. The answer key begins on page 119.

### Day-by-Day Skills List

This list indicates the skills involved in each separate daily problem. It can help you pinpoint and analyze students' strengths and weaknesses. It begins on page 123.

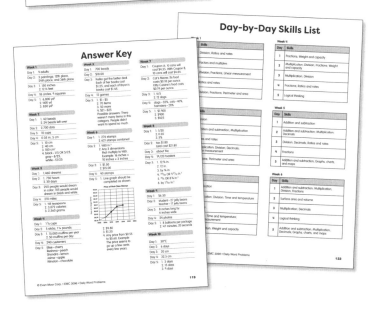

# How to Use This Book

1. Reproduce and distribute How to Solve Word Problems on page 7. Use the page to walk your class through the first several problems, using think-alouds to model the Read, Think, and Draw steps.

2. Reproduce and cut apart the problems for each five-day week, or distribute a student book to each student.

3. Preview the page yourself before assigning it to the class. Provide support if there is vocabulary or a concept that students might not be familiar with.

4. Have students work independently, with a partner, or as a class.

   • Remind students that there are usually multiple ways to solve problems. Several of the problems are open-ended and do not have a single correct answer.

   • Students may take some time to figure out how to start; productive struggle is part of the learning process. Guide students with leading questions if needed.

5. Allow time for sharing solutions and problem-solving strategies. Modeling a variety of approaches broadens learning and encourages peer respect and cooperation.

## Our Approach

Math exists to solve real-world problems. We encounter many of these problems every day: how much purchases will cost, how long before the school bus arrives, how many eggs are needed for 5 batches of cookies. These problems are not written out for us—they just arise. No one says, "This is going to be an addition problem" or "You'll have to calculate the total needed first and then subtract what you already have." We figure this out from the context and information at hand.

Solving problems, mathematical and otherwise, requires reasoning. The main purpose of word problems is to practice translating the situations in problems into mathematical language. This translation must take place within the context of the problem and show the relationship of the amounts to each other. The problem solver must understand the context and the goal and determine what information is known and what is unknown.

The problems in this book are written as authentically as possible, without intentionally embedding key words as clues to the appropriate operations. Doing so would deprive students of the visualization and analysis practice required to solve real-life problems. Shortcuts for approaching certain types of problems may appear to save time and effort, but they require a lot of memory in the long run, as there are infinite types of problems.

By supporting the higher-order thinking aspects of problem solving, we are teaching students to be thinkers and doers and to believe in their abilities as problem solvers.

# How to Solve Word Problems

Word problems are math stories about things that can happen every day in real life. Every problem is different. There is no single way to solve all problems. You need to put yourself in the picture to understand each situation. After you understand what is going on, you can figure out what you need to solve any problem in a math class or in real life.

**Read**

**Read for the basic idea:** Read the problem once to see what it's about.

**Ask yourself:** What's going on in the situation?

**Think**

**Read the problem again more carefully:** Put yourself in the situation. Think about the details. Decide what you need to figure out.

**Ask yourself:** What is the goal of the problem?

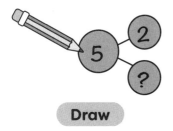

**Draw**

**Draw a picture, diagram, or model of the situation:** Each important number should be included, as well as the part you are trying to figure out.

**Ask yourself:** What do these numbers have to do with each other?

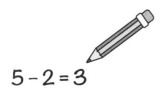

$5 - 2 = 3$

**Solve**

**Solve the problem:** Decide which operation or operations you need. You can write an equation to help you solve it. **Hint:** Sometimes there will be several steps needed to reach the goal of the problem.

**Ask yourself:** What do I need to add, subtract, multiply, or divide? Do I need to figure out another number first?

**Check**

**Check your answer:** Put your answer in your picture or diagram.

**Ask yourself:** Does my response answer the question? Does it make sense?

# Scope and Sequence

| Week | 1 | 2 | 3 | 4 | 5 | 6 | 7 | 8 | 9 | 10 | 11 | 12 | 13 | 14 | 15 | 16 | 17 | 18 |
|---|---|---|---|---|---|---|---|---|---|---|---|---|---|---|---|---|---|---|
| Positive and negative numbers | | | | | | | | | | ● | ● | | ● | | ● | | ● | ● |
| Addition and subtraction | | ● | | | ● | ● | ● | ● | ● | ● | ● | ● | ● | ● | | | ● | ● |
| Multiplication | | ● | ● | ● | ● | ● | ● | ● | ● | ● | ● | ● | ● | ● | | ● | | ● |
| Division | ● | ● | ● | ● | ● | ● | ● | ● | ● | | ● | ● | ● | ● | ● | | | ● |
| Factors and multiples | ● | | | | | | | | ● | | | | | | | | | |
| Fractions | ● | ● | ● | ● | ● | ● | ● | ● | | | | | ● | | | | ● | |
| Decimals | | ● | | | ● | ● | ● | ● | ● | ● | ● | ● | | ● | ● | ● | | ● |
| Percents | | | | | | | ● | ● | ● | ● | | | ● | ● | ● | | | |
| Ratios and rates | ● | ● | | ● | ● | | ● | ● | | | ● | ● | | ● | | ● | | |
| Expressions and equations | | | | | | | | | | | | | ● | | | | ● | ● |
| Inequalities | | | | | | | | | | | | | | | | | | |
| Time and temperature | | | ● | | | | | | ● | | | ● | ● | | ● | | | ● |
| Linear measurement | ● | ● | ● | | | | | | | | ● | ● | | | | | | ● |
| Weight and capacity | | | | ● | ● | | | | | | | | | | | | | |
| Perimeter and area | ● | ● | | | | | | ● | ● | | | | | | ● | | ● | |
| Surface area and volume | | | | | | ● | | | | | | | | | | | ● | |
| Statistics | | | | | | | | | | | | | | ● | | | | |
| Coordinate plane | | | | | | | | | | | | | | | | ● | | |
| Graphs, charts, and maps | | | | | ● | ● | ● | | | ● | | | | | ● | | ● | |
| Logical thinking | | | | ● | | ● | | | | | | | ● | | | | ● | |
| Spatial reasoning | | | | | | | | | | | ● | | | | | | ● | ● |

Daily Word Problems • EMC 3096 • © Evan-Moor Corp.

| 19 | 20 | 21 | 22 | 23 | 24 | 25 | 26 | 27 | 28 | 29 | 30 | 31 | 32 | 33 | 34 | 35 | 36 | Week |
|---|---|---|---|---|---|---|---|---|---|---|---|---|---|---|---|---|---|---|
|  |  |  |  |  |  |  | ● | ● |  | ● |  |  |  |  |  | ● |  | Positive and negative numbers |
| ● |  | ● | ● | ● | ● |  | ● | ● |  | ● |  |  | ● | ● | ● |  | ● | Addition and subtraction |
|  | ● | ● |  | ● | ● | ● | ● | ● |  | ● | ● |  | ● |  | ● | ● | ● | Multiplication |
| ● | ● | ● |  | ● | ● | ● |  | ● |  |  |  |  |  |  | ● |  | ● | Division |
|  | ● |  |  | ● |  |  |  |  |  |  | ● |  |  |  |  | ● |  | Factors and multiples |
|  | ● |  |  |  | ● | ● | ● |  |  | ● | ● | ● |  | ● | ● |  |  | Fractions |
| ● |  |  |  |  | ● |  | ● |  |  |  |  |  |  |  |  | ● | ● | Decimals |
|  |  | ● |  | ● |  |  | ● | ● |  | ● |  |  | ● |  |  |  |  | Percents |
| ● |  | ● | ● |  |  | ● |  |  |  |  |  | ● |  | ● | ● | ● | ● | Ratios and rates |
| ● |  |  |  |  | ● |  |  |  |  |  |  |  |  |  |  |  |  | Expressions and equations |
|  |  | ● | ● | ● | ● |  |  |  |  | ● |  |  |  | ● |  |  |  | Inequalities |
| ● |  |  |  |  |  |  |  |  |  |  |  |  | ● |  |  |  |  | Time and temperature |
|  |  |  |  |  |  | ● |  |  |  |  |  | ● |  |  |  | ● | ● | Linear measurement |
|  | ● |  |  |  |  |  |  |  |  |  |  | ● |  |  |  |  |  | Weight and capacity |
|  | ● |  | ● |  |  | ● | ● |  | ● |  |  |  |  |  |  |  |  | Perimeter and area |
|  |  | ● |  |  | ● | ● |  | ● |  |  |  | ● |  | ● |  |  |  | Surface area and volume |
| ● | ● |  |  |  |  |  | ● |  |  | ● |  | ● | ● |  | ● |  | ● | Statistics |
|  |  | ● |  | ● |  |  |  |  | ● |  |  |  |  |  |  |  |  | Coordinate plane |
| ● |  |  |  |  |  |  |  | ● |  | ● |  | ● |  |  | ● | ● |  | Graphs, charts, and maps |
|  |  |  |  |  |  |  |  |  |  |  | ● |  |  | ● |  | ● |  | Logical thinking |
|  | ● |  | ● |  |  |  |  |  | ● |  | ● |  |  | ● |  | ● | ● | Spatial reasoning |

Name _____

# My Progress

How many did I get correct each week? Make a bar graph.

| | | | | | | |
|---|---|---|---|---|---|---|
| 5 | | | | | | |
| 4 | | | | | | |
| 3 | | | | | | |
| 2 | | | | | | |
| 1 | | | | | | |

Week ___   Week ___   Week ___   Week ___   Week ___   Week ___

1. A skill that I did well was _____.

2. A skill that I need to practice is _____.

- - - - - - - - - - - - - - - - - - - - - - - - - - - - - - - - - - - - ✂ - - - - - - - -

Name _____

# My Progress

How many did I get correct each week? Make a bar graph.

| | | | | | | |
|---|---|---|---|---|---|---|
| 5 | | | | | | |
| 4 | | | | | | |
| 3 | | | | | | |
| 2 | | | | | | |
| 1 | | | | | | |

Week ___   Week ___   Week ___   Week ___   Week ___   Week ___

1. A skill that I did well was _____.

2. A skill that I need to practice is _____.

# Daily Word Problems

WEEK 1 • DAY 1

**Art Museum**

Name: _____

Some sixth-grade classes were going on a field trip to the Picture-Perfect Art Museum. The school required 1 adult chaperone for every 15 students.

If there were 135 students going on the field trip, how many adults were needed?

Work Space:

Answer:

_____ adults

---

# Daily Word Problems

WEEK 1 • DAY 2

**Art Museum**

Name: _____

The art museum had an exhibit named "Flower Power." Each of the 36 paintings featured colorful flowers. The paintings were hung in one row. The 12th painting had white, blue, and yellow flowers. Every 3rd painting after that had white flowers, every 4th one had blue flowers, and every 6th one had yellow flowers.

How many paintings in all had all three colors of flowers? In which places were those paintings in the row?

Work Space:

Answer:

_____ paintings had all three colors

and appeared in _____

_____ place in the row.

# Daily Word Problems

## WEEK 1 • DAY 3

**Art Museum**

Name: _____

Damien's friend Darryl took a picture of Damien standing next to a huge sculpture of a lion. Darryl said, "Wow! That lion is $2\frac{1}{2}$ times as tall as you are!"

1. If Damien is 60 inches tall, how many inches tall was the sculpture?

2. How many feet is that?

Work Space:

Answer:

1. _____ inches

2. _____ feet

---

# Daily Word Problems

## WEEK 1 • DAY 4

**Art Museum**

Name: _____

The Picture-Perfect Art Museum displayed a large mobile that was made up of circles and squares. The ratio of circles to squares was 2 to 1.

The mobile had 27 shapes in all. How many circles and squares were there?

Work Space:

Answer:

_____ circles

_____ squares

# Daily Word Problems

## WEEK 1 • DAY 5

**Art Museum**

The Picture-Perfect Art Museum has the following floor plan:

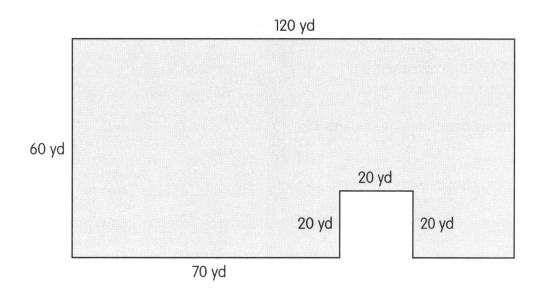

120 yd

60 yd

20 yd

20 yd

20 yd

70 yd

1. What is the area of the museum? _____ yd²

2. What is the perimeter of the museum? _____ yd

3. If the museum built an additional wing that was $\frac{1}{8}$ the size of the current building, what would be the area of the new wing? _____ yd²

# Daily Word Problems

## WEEK 2 • DAY 1

**Arts and Crafts**

The art teacher had a container of 1,200 beads. She divided the beads among her 28 students for an art project. All the students received an equal number of beads.

1. How many beads did the students receive?

2. How many beads were left over?

Work Space:

Answer:

1. _____ beads

2. _____ beads left over

---

# Daily Word Problems

## WEEK 2 • DAY 2

**Arts and Crafts**

Danielle used a technique called *pointillism* in art class. She painted tiny dots of color on a canvas to create a picture of a dog.

Danielle painted 450 white dots. She painted twice as many black dots and three times as many brown dots. How many dots were in Danielle's picture?

Work Space:

Answer:

_____ dots

Name: _____

## Daily Word Problems

**WEEK 2 • DAY 3**

**Arts and Crafts**

Tanisha decided to make some ceramic cups in pottery class. She wanted to make a set to give to her mom.

Tanisha made 6 cups in 3 days. If she worked at the same pace, how many cups could she make in 5 days?

Work Space:

Answer:

_____ cups

---

Name: _____

## Daily Word Problems

**WEEK 2 • DAY 4**

**Arts and Crafts**

Aiden glued toothpicks together to make a model of a boat. After he finished, he measured his model. It was 0.45 meter from one end to the other.

If Aiden's boat measured 9 toothpicks from one end to the other, how long was each toothpick? Give the answer in both meters and centimeters.

Work Space:

Answer:

_____ m

_____ cm

# Daily Word Problems
## WEEK 2 • DAY 5

**Arts and Crafts**

Lin glued square tiles together to make a mosaic. The squares were black, gray, and white. Each tile had sides that were 2 cm long.

1. Look at this part of the mosaic. What is the length of each side?  _____ cm

2. What is the perimeter of the mosaic?  _____ cm

3. What is the area of the mosaic?  _____ cm$^2$

4. What fraction of the mosaic is each color?

   black  _____

   gray  _____

   white  _____

Name: _____

## Daily Word Problems

**Sweet Dreams**

### WEEK 3 • DAY 1

Janna learned that a person has at least 4 dreams per night. Janna said, "That's a lot dreams! That means a person has 20 dreams every 5 nights!"

How many dreams would a person have in a year?

Work Space:

Answer:

_____ dreams

---

Name: _____

## Daily Word Problems

**Sweet Dreams**

### WEEK 3 • DAY 2

Leo read that most people dream for 2 hours every night. "I wonder how many hours a person dreams in one whole year," thought Leo.

1. What is the total number of hours a person dreams in a year?

2. About how many 24-hour days would that be?

Work Space:

Answer:

1. _____ hours

2. _____ days

# Daily Word Problems

## WEEK 3 • DAY 3

**Sweet Dreams**

Some researchers found that $\frac{7}{10}$ of the population dreams in color, while the rest dreams in black and white.

Suppose there were 350 people sleeping at a hotel. According to the above information, how many people would dream in color, and how many would dream in black and white?

Work Space:

Answer:

_____ people would dream in color.

_____ people would dream in black and white.

---

# Daily Word Problems

## WEEK 3 • DAY 4

**Sweet Dreams**

In the movie *The Wizard of Oz*, a tornado picks up a farmhouse and carries a girl named Dorothy to a magical land called Oz. At the end of the story, Dorothy finds out that everything was a dream!

The speed of a tornado strong enough to lift a house reaches 315 miles per hour. Suppose the wind blew that fast in a straight line for 40 minutes. How far would it have carried Dorothy's house?

Work Space:

Answer:

_____ miles

Name: _____

# Daily Word Problems

## WEEK 3 • DAY 5

**Sweet Dreams**

In the film *Winnie the Pooh,* a little bear dreams about a land where everything is made of honey. Pooh dreams about eating honey, swimming in a river of honey, and dancing with bears made of honey!

Use the charts to help you solve the problems.

| **Liquid Honey** |
| --- |
| 1 serving: 1 tablespoon |
| calories    64 |
| sugar        16 grams |

1. Pooh loves honey so much that he can easily eat several jars a day. If one of his jars held 1 cup of honey, how many teaspoons would that be?

_____ teaspoons

| 3 teaspoons = 1 tablespoon |
| --- |
| 16 tablespoons = 1 cup |

2. If Pooh dreamed of eating 3 jarfuls of honey, how many calories would that be?

_____ calories

3. If a bear in Pooh's dream were made of 10 cups of honey, how many grams of sugar would that bear consist of?

_____ grams

Name: _____

## Daily Word Problems

### WEEK 4 • DAY 1

**Bo's Bakery**

Bo the Baker makes the best cookies! His recipe for Triple-Chip Cookies uses $\frac{1}{2}$ cup of chocolate chips, $\frac{3}{4}$ cup of butterscotch chips, and $\frac{5}{8}$ cup of peanut butter chips. Yum!

How many cups of chips does Bo use to make one batch of Triple-Chip Cookies?

Work Space:

Answer:

_____ cups

---

Name: _____

## Daily Word Problems

### WEEK 4 • DAY 2

**Bo's Bakery**

Bo the Baker buys butter that comes in sticks. Four sticks are equal to 1 pound of butter. Each stick is equal to $\frac{1}{2}$ cup.

One of Bo's best-selling items is his Super-Flaky Butter Biscuits. He uses $\frac{1}{4}$ cup of butter for each batch. Each batch makes 12 biscuits. If Bo makes 120 biscuits, how many sticks of butter does he use? How many pounds of butter is that?

Work Space:

Answer:

_____ sticks

_____ pounds

Name: _____

# Daily Word Problems

**Bo's Bakery**

## WEEK 4 • DAY 3

Bo the Baker makes marvelous muffins. They're so popular that he averages 1,250 muffin sales a month.

1. At that rate, how many muffins would Bo sell in a year?

2. If Bo's Bakery is open 300 days a year, how many muffins does Bo sell on average per day?

Work Space:

Answer:

1. _____ muffins per year

2. _____ muffins per day

---

Name: _____

# Daily Word Problems

**Bo's Bakery**

## WEEK 4 • DAY 4

Bo kept track of his cookie sales. He discovered that 3 out of 5 people who came into his bakery for cookies bought chocolate chip cookies.

If 400 customers bought cookies at Bo's Bakery last month, how many of them bought chocolate chip cookies?

Work Space:

Answer:

_____ customers

# Daily Word Problems

## WEEK 4 • DAY 5

**Bo's Bakery**

Bo's Bakery is known for its delicious pies. Read the clues and fill in the chart to determine what kind of pie each customer bought. When you know that a name and a pie do **not** go together, make an **X** under that pie and across from that name. When you know that a name and a pie **do** go together, write **YES** in that box.

**Clues:**

- Jaime bought apple or chocolate.
- Reshma did not buy cherry or chocolate.
- Elise and Shondra bought a fruit pie.
- Winston and Shondra did not buy apple or cherry.
- Elise and Winston did not buy peach or lemon.
- Shondra is allergic to peaches and never buys them.

|  | apple | peach | cherry | lemon | chocolate |
|---|---|---|---|---|---|
| **Elise** |  |  |  |  |  |
| **Reshma** |  |  |  |  |  |
| **Shondra** |  |  |  |  |  |
| **Jaime** |  |  |  |  |  |
| **Winston** |  |  |  |  |  |

Write the correct flavor beside each name.

Elise _____    Jaime _____

Reshma _____    Winston _____

Shondra _____

Name: _____

# Daily Word Problems

## WEEK 5 • DAY 1

**Garage Sale**

Luisa bought a bag of beads at a garage sale. When she got home, she counted the beads. There were 125 blue beads and twice as many yellow beads. There were also 75 more red beads than yellow beads.

How many beads did Luisa buy at the garage sale?

Work Space:

Answer:

_____ beads

---

Name: _____

# Daily Word Problems

## WEEK 5 • DAY 2

**Garage Sale**

Benjamin brought his nickel jar to a garage sale. It contained 322 nickels. He found a bike he wanted, but he would need 38 more nickels to buy it.

How much did the bike cost?

Work Space:

Answer:

$_____

Name: _____

# Daily Word Problems

**WEEK 5 • DAY 3**

**Garage Sale**

Keiko and Bryan each bought some Harry Potter books at a garage sale. Keiko bought 5 books at Ms. Lozano's garage sale for $6.25. Bryan bought 4 books for $5.80 at Mr. Rogan's garage sale.

Who got the better deal? Explain why.

Work Space:

Answer:

_____

_____

_____

_____

_____

---

Name: _____

# Daily Word Problems

**WEEK 5 • DAY 4**

**Garage Sale**

Rashid wanted to sell some of his board games at his family's garage sale. He set them out on a table. At the end of the day, he figured out how many were sold.

Rashid said, "I sold 9 games. That's $\frac{3}{4}$ of all the games that were for sale." How many board games were for sale at the beginning of the day?

Work Space:

Answer:

_____ games

# Daily Word Problems

## WEEK 5 • DAY 5

**Garage Sale**

Some families had a neighborhood garage sale. They priced the items between $1 and $25. The histogram shows how many items in the different price categories were sold.

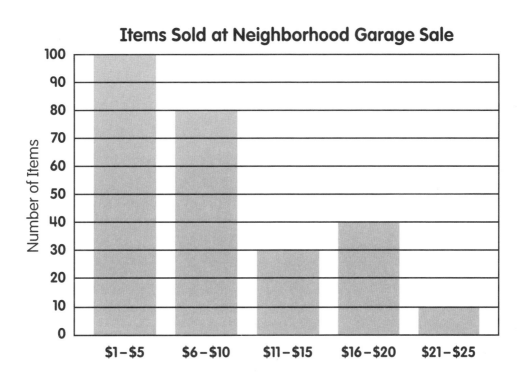

**Items Sold at Neighborhood Garage Sale**

1. In which price category were the most items sold? _____

2. How many items that cost between $11 and $20 were sold? _____ items

3. How many more items were sold in the $6–$10 price range than in the $11–$15 price range? _____ more

4. In which price category were the fewest items sold?  _____

   What is one possible reason that this happened?

   _____

   _____

   _____

Name: _____

# Daily Word Problems

## WEEK 6 • DAY 1

**Stamp Collections**

Caleb and Leia collect stamps. Caleb has 345 stamps in his collection. Leia has $\frac{4}{5}$ the number of stamps that Caleb has.

1. How many stamps does Leia have?

2. How many stamps do Caleb and Leia have combined?

Work Space:

Answer:

1. _____ stamps

2. _____ stamps combined

---

Name: _____

# Daily Word Problems

## WEEK 6 • DAY 2

**Stamp Collections**

Daisuke keeps his stamp collection in a box that is 12 inches long, 10 inches wide, and 4 inches tall.

1. What is the volume of the box?

2. Daisuke's friend Quinn keeps her stamp collection in a box that has the same volume as Daisuke's box but different dimensions. What could be the dimensions of Quinn's box?

Work Space:

Answer:

1. _____ in.³

2. _____

_____

# Daily Word Problems

## WEEK 6 • DAY 3

**Stamp Collections**

Alana has a 1916 stamp in her collection that cost $0.03 when it was first issued. Now the stamp is worth 50 times as much!

1. How much is the stamp worth now?

2. Alana found out that if her 1916 stamp were in perfect condition, it would be worth 500 times its original value. How much would that be?

Work Space:

Answer:

1. $_____

2. $_____

---

# Daily Word Problems

## WEEK 6 • DAY 4

**Stamp Collections**

Travis decided to keep only stamps that feature pictures of athletes. Last week he sold half of his collection to his friend Dana. Then Travis bought 10 more stamps. Now he has 30 in his collection.

How many stamps did Travis have before he sold some to Dana?

Work Space:

Answer:

_____ stamps

Name: _____

# Daily Word Problems

## WEEK 6 • DAY 5

**Stamp Collections**

Matt started collecting stamps in 2002. Each year, he bought a sheet of new stamps. The cost depended on the price of a single stamp. For example, in 2002 a first-class stamp to mail a letter cost $0.37. A sheet of 20 of those stamps cost $7.40.

The table shows the prices of postage stamps over the years.

1. Use the information in the table to complete the line graph.

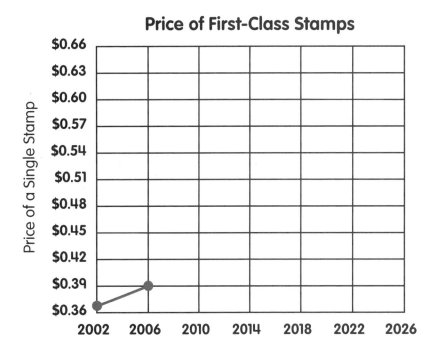

| Year | Price of Stamp |
|------|----------------|
| 2002 | $0.37 |
| 2006 | $0.39 |
| 2010 | $0.44 |
| 2014 | $0.49 |
| 2018 | $0.50 |

2. How much did Matt pay for a sheet of 20 stamps in 2014?          $_____

3. How much more did he pay for 20 stamps in 2018 than in 2010?          $_____

4. Based on the graph, what do you think a stamp will probably cost in 2026? Explain.

_____

_____

Name: _____

# Daily Word Problems

## WEEK 7 • DAY 1

**Penelope's Pet Parlor**

Jin needs to buy cat food. She has two coupons from Penelope's Pet Parlor.

**Coupon A**

KITTY CUISINE
SPECIAL
Buy 1, get a 2nd
one for 50% off!

**Coupon B**

KITTY CUISINE
SALE
Buy 8,
Get 2 FREE!

Jin will buy 10 cans of Kitty Cuisine. Each can usually costs $0.58. Which coupon offers the best value? Explain.

Work Space:

Answer:

_____

_____

_____

_____

_____

---

Name: _____

# Daily Word Problems

## WEEK 7 • DAY 2

**Penelope's Pet Parlor**

Jin is thinking of switching from Kitty Cuisine to Cat's Meow. Before she decides, she wants to compare prices. At Penelope's Pet Parlor, Kitty Cuisine cat food is sold in 3-oz. cans that cost $0.58 each. Cat's Meow is sold in 5.5-oz. cans that cost $0.99 each.

Which brand offers the better buy? Explain.

Work Space:

Answer:

_____

_____

_____

Name: _____

# Daily Word Problems

## WEEK 7 • DAY 3

**Penelope's Pet Parlor**

Liam went to Penelope's Pet Parlor to buy a pet. He noticed that there were 16 dogs and 20 cats.

1. What was the ratio of dogs to cats? Write your answer as a fraction in lowest terms.

2. Suppose the ratio of dogs to cats always stayed the same. If there were 15 cats, how many dogs would there be?

Work Space:

Answer:

1. _____

2. _____ dogs

---

Name: _____

# Daily Word Problems

## WEEK 7 • DAY 4

**Penelope's Pet Parlor**

Penelope's Pet Parlor had a sale and found homes for many of its animals. On Friday, the shop sold 8 dogs, 10 cats, and 7 hamsters.

What percent of the total sales came from dogs? What percent came from cats? What percent came from hamsters?

Work Space:

Answer:

dogs _____%

cats _____%

hamsters _____%

Name: _____

# Daily Word Problems

## WEEK 7 • DAY 5

**Penelope's Pet Parlor**

The graph shows the income and expenses for four weeks at Penelope's Pet Parlor.

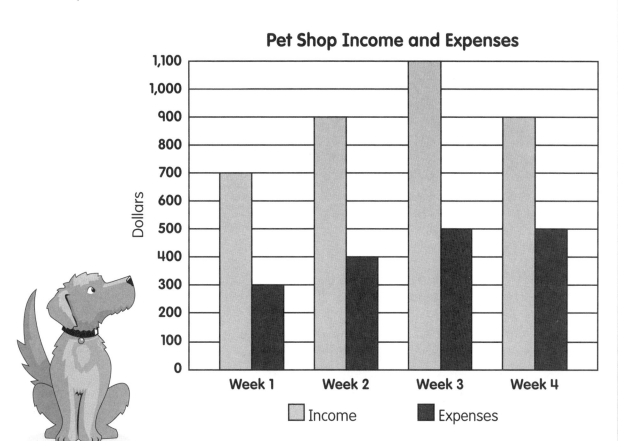

**Pet Shop Income and Expenses**

1. What was the profit for the four weeks?
   (Hint: Profit is income minus expenses.)          $_____

2. What was the average income for the four weeks?   $_____

3. What were the average expenses for the four weeks?   $_____

© Evan-Moor Corp. • EMC 3096 • *Daily Word Problems*                                31

# Daily Word Problems

## WEEK 8 • DAY 1

**Baseball Cards**

Name: _____

A box of 200 baseball cards included 10 cards that featured the Los Angeles Dodgers.

1. What fraction of the cards featured the L.A. Dodgers? Use simplest form.

2. What is this amount as a decimal?

3. What percent of the cards featured the L.A. Dodgers?

Work Space:

Answer:

1. _____

2. _____

3. _____%

---

# Daily Word Problems

## WEEK 8 • DAY 2

**Baseball Cards**

Name: _____

One store was selling a box of baseball cards for $20. If you had to pay 9% sales tax on the item, how much would the tax be? What would be the total cost of the baseball cards?

Work Space:

Answer:

tax: $_____

total cost: $_____

## Daily Word Problems

**WEEK 8 • DAY 3**

**Baseball Cards**

Name: _____

Work Space:

In the 1950s, baseball cards were sold in packs of 5, along with a free piece of chewing gum. A pack cost a nickel back then. That means each card cost only a penny!

In 2018, a pack of 7 baseball cards cost a dollar. About how much did one card cost based on this rate?

Answer:

about _____¢

---

## Daily Word Problems

**WEEK 8 • DAY 4**

**Baseball Cards**

Name: _____

Work Space:

The Topps Chewing Gum Company began producing baseball cards in the 1950s. Topps gave gifts to the ballplayers in exchange for the right to use their pictures. Willie Mays, a well-known player, received a toaster one year.

In 2016, a 1952 Willie Mays rookie card from Topps sold for $478,000! Currently, a toaster may cost $25. How many toasters could you buy with the money spent on the Willie Mays rookie card?

Answer:

_____ toasters

# Daily Word Problems

## WEEK 8 • DAY 5

**Baseball Cards**

Most baseball cards today measure $2\frac{1}{2}$ inches by $3\frac{1}{2}$ inches. That's the size of a wallet-size photograph. But baseball cards weren't always that size. From 1952 to 1956, the Topps Company made cards that measured $2\frac{5}{8}$ inches by $3\frac{3}{4}$ inches. Then they changed the size to what we see today.

1. What was the perimeter of the old cards? _____ in.

2. What was the perimeter of the new cards? _____ in.

3. How much did the perimeter decrease?

   It decreased by _____ in.

4. What was the area of the old cards? _____ in.²

5. What was the area of the new cards? _____ in.²

6. How much did the area decrease?

   It decreased by _____ in.²

   Daily Word Problems • EMC 3096 • © Evan-Moor Corp.

Name: _____

# Daily Word Problems

## WEEK 9 • DAY 1

**Happy Birthday!**

Mr. Lee bought party favors for his daughter's birthday party. He divided the favors equally into 15 treat bags for the guests.

Mr. Lee spent a total of $97.50. How much did he spend on each bag?

Work Space:

Answer:

$_____

---

Name: _____

# Daily Word Problems

## WEEK 9 • DAY 2

**Happy Birthday!**

Ellie brought a jar of jelly beans to school to share with her class for her birthday. There were 800 jelly beans in the jar. Ellie divided the jelly beans equally among the 29 students and gave the leftovers to the teacher.

How many jelly beans did Ellie give each student? How many did the teacher receive?

Work Space:

Answer:

Each student got _____ jelly beans.

The teacher got _____ jelly beans.

# Daily Word Problems

## WEEK 9 • DAY 3

**Happy Birthday!**

Jake received a birthday card from his grandparents. The length of the card was 2 inches longer than the width. The card had an area of 48 square inches.

What were the dimensions of the card?

Work Space:

Answer:

_____ inches long by

_____ inches wide

---

# Daily Word Problems

## WEEK 9 • DAY 4

**Happy Birthday!**

Kareem's mom took digital photos of Kareem's birthday party. She displayed them on a large bulletin board for the guests to enjoy.

Kareem appeared in 60% of the photos. There were 40 photos in all. How many featured Kareem?

Work Space:

Answer:

_____ photos

# Daily Word Problems

## WEEK 9 • DAY 5

**Happy Birthday!**

Cailey is excited about her "Awesome 80s Birthday Bash" that's coming up next week. Read about some of the things she has done to get ready for her party. Then answer the questions.

1. Cailey bought packages of neon-colored balloons for her party. The balloons in each package were all the same color. Each package contained the same number of balloons. Cailey bought 24 pink balloons, 32 yellow balloons, and 40 green balloons. What was the greatest number of balloons that could have been in each package?

   _____ balloons per package

2. Cailey put together a recording of 80s music to play at her party. She recorded a total of 15 songs. Each song lasted 3 minutes, with a 10-second break between songs. How long was the recording?

   _____ minutes, _____ seconds

Name: _____

# Daily Word Problems

## WEEK 10 • DAY 1

**Wacky Weather**

Wacky Town's weather is unpredictable! The temperature last Friday was a warm 18°C at noon. By 7:00 p.m., the temperature had dropped to –12°C, and a freezing hailstorm started!

How much did the temperature drop between noon and 7:00 p.m.?

Work Space:

Answer:

_____ °C

---

Name: _____

# Daily Word Problems

## WEEK 10 • DAY 2

**Wacky Weather**

Last year, Wacky Town had strange weather in the month of April. Instead of the usual spring sunshine, there was snowfall on 20% of the days!

There are 30 days in April. On how many days did it snow?

Work Space:

Answer:

_____ days

Name: _____

# Daily Word Problems

**WEEK 10 • DAY 3**

**Wacky Weather**

One year, a huge hailstone fell right in the middle of Wacky Town. A typical hailstone measures about 2.5 cm across, but this one was 8 times that size!

What was the size of Wacky Town's huge hailstone?

Work Space:

Answer:

The hailstone measured

_____ cm across.

---

Name: _____

# Daily Word Problems

**WEEK 10 • DAY 4**

**Wacky Weather**

When the people of Wacky Town talk about their unusual weather, they sometimes ask, "Remember December?" That's because there was a strange snowfall pattern one December. It snowed 1 cm on the 1st day, 1.5 cm on the 2nd, 2 cm on the 3rd, 2.5 cm on the 4th, and so on for 10 days!

How much snow fell during those 10 days?

Work Space:

Answer:

_____ cm

**Wacky Weather**

Wacky Town gets all kinds of weather during the 30 days of November. Some days are warm and sunny. Others are gray and cloudy. Some days are rainy, while others are snowy! The circle graph shows the percentage of days that were sunny, cloudy, snowy, and rainy last November.

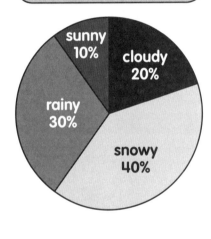

**Wacky Town's November Weather**

sunny 10%
cloudy 20%
rainy 30%
snowy 40%

1. How many days were sunny?

   _____ days

2. How many days were rainy or cloudy?

   _____ days

3. How many more days were snowy than sunny?

   _____ days

Daily Word Problems • EMC 3096 • © Evan-Moor Corp.

## Daily Word Problems

**WEEK 11 • DAY 1**

**Food Drive**

Name: _____

The students of Happyvale School collected 2,250 cans of food during their food drive. They also helped pack the cans into boxes to take to a nearby food bank.

Each box held 48 cans. How many boxes were needed for all of the donated cans?

Work Space:

Answer:

_____ boxes

---

## Daily Word Problems

**WEEK 11 • DAY 2**

**Food Drive**

Name: _____

Jee's family donated 3 cases of soup for her school's food drive. Each case had 3 rows of 4 soup cans. Each can contained 14.75 ounces of soup.

How many ounces of soup did Jee's family donate in all?

Work Space:

Answer:

_____ ounces

Name: _____

# Daily Word Problems

**WEEK 11 • DAY 3**

**Food Drive**

The students at Reni's school collected cans of fruits and vegetables for their food drive. There were 300 cans in all.

Three out of every 5 cans were vegetables. How many of the 300 cans contained vegetables? How many contained fruit?

Work Space:

Answer:

vegetables: _____ cans

fruit: _____ cans

---

Name: _____

# Daily Word Problems

**WEEK 11 • DAY 4**

**Food Drive**

Ms. Walsh works at a food pantry. She keeps track of the food that comes in and goes out each day. Donated items are recorded as positive numbers. Items distributed to needy families are recorded as negative numbers.

The food pantry started with 500 food items. How many items were there after the following donations and distributions?

+20, −45, −30, +10, −12

Work Space:

Answer:

_____ food items

Name: _____

# Daily Word Problems

## WEEK 11 • DAY 5

**Food Drive**

A local food pantry collected canned goods and stored them in a large cupboard. Each shelf in the cupboard is 28 inches long, 11 inches deep, and 10 inches tall. Each can is 3 inches across and $4\frac{1}{2}$ inches tall.

1. How many cans would fit in a single layer and in a single row along the length of one shelf?

   _____ cans

2. How many cans would fit in a single layer on the entire base of one shelf?

   _____ cans

3. Suppose the cans were stacked one on top of the other. What is the maximum number of cans that could be stored on one shelf?

   _____ cans

Name: _____

# Daily Word Problems

## WEEK 12 • DAY 1

**Car Racing**

Sergio finished the car race in 1 hour, 38 minutes, 15 seconds. Conor finished 0.09 second faster than Sergio. Jules finished 0.2 second faster than Conor.

How long did it take Jules to finish the race?

Work Space:

Answer:

_____

---

Name: _____

# Daily Word Problems

## WEEK 12 • DAY 2

**Car Racing**

Nigel changed the aluminum body on his race car to a more lightweight material called carbon fiber. This let him drive his car 10% farther on a tank of gas.

Nigel was able to travel 480 miles on a tank of gas with the old aluminum body. How many miles was he able to travel on a tank of gas with the new carbon fiber body?

Work Space:

Answer:

_____ miles

Name: _____

# Daily Word Problems

**Car Racing**

## WEEK 12 • DAY 3

Alicia's race car is really quick! It can go from 0 miles an hour (standing still) to 190 miles an hour in 10 seconds. In that same amount of time, her regular family car reaches only 63 miles an hour.

About how many times faster is Alicia's race car than her family car?

Work Space:

Answer:

about _____ times faster

---

Name: _____

# Daily Word Problems

**Car Racing**

## WEEK 12 • DAY 4

During a practice race, Mario's average time for completing a lap was 1 minute, 15 seconds. Danica's average lap time was 1 minute, 12 seconds. The practice race was 80 laps.

Who won the race? By how many minutes did that person win?

Work Space:

Answer:

_____ won the

race by _____ minutes.

# Daily Word Problems

## WEEK 12 • DAY 5

**Car Racing**

The Fearsome Five Racing Series is made up of five races. Only five drivers enter the race, and the same five compete throughout the series.

The table on the left shows the results of the races completed so far. Each number gives the driver's finishing position. For example, Driver E came in 4th in Race 1. The table on the right shows the points drivers can earn in a race. For example, the driver who comes in 1st earns 7 points, while the driver who comes in 2nd earns 4.

**Race Results – Finishing Positions**

| Driver | Race 1 | Race 2 | Race 3 | Race 4 | Race 5 | Points |
|--------|--------|--------|--------|--------|--------|--------|
| A | 1 | 1 | 2 | | | 18 |
| B | 2 | 3 | 1 | | | |
| C | 3 | 2 | 3 | | | |
| D | 5 | 4 | 4 | | | |
| E | 4 | 5 | 5 | | | |

**Points**

| Finishing Position | Points Awarded |
|--------------------|----------------|
| 1st | 7 |
| 2nd | 4 |
| 3rd | 2 |
| 4th | 1 |
| 5th | 0 |

The driver with the most points after all five races are completed wins the championship. Fill in the Points column in the Race Results table to show the points the drivers have earned so far.

Do all five drivers have a chance at winning the championship? Explain.

_____

_____

_____

_____

_____

# Daily Word Problems

## WEEK 13 • DAY 1

**Vacations**

There are 96 sixth-grade students at one school. During summer vacation, $\frac{3}{4}$ of the sixth graders will be taking a trip. Of those students traveling, $\frac{3}{8}$ will be going out of the country.

How many students will be spending summer vacation in another country?

Work Space:

Answer:

_____ students

---

# Daily Word Problems

## WEEK 13 • DAY 2

**Vacations**

During summer vacation, Alberto is planning to take his 8 cousins to a water park near his house. The entrance fee for the park is $16 per person. Luckily, the park will have a summer special. Groups of 8 people or more receive a 10% discount on the fee.

How much will Alberto need to pay for himself and his cousins?

Work Space:

Answer:

$_____

# Daily Word Problems

**WEEK 13 • DAY 3**

**Vacations**

Althea and her family are driving to Funtastic City for a vacation. They drove $\frac{1}{4}$ of the way and stopped for lunch. Then they traveled another $\frac{3}{8}$ of the way before stopping at a hotel for the night.

What fraction of the total distance do they still need to travel to reach Funtastic City?

Work Space:

Answer:

_____ of the total distance

---

# Daily Word Problems

**WEEK 13 • DAY 4**

**Vacations**

Maher's family is planning a ski trip. Here is what he found when he looked up the average temperatures of one ski resort:

| | |
|---|---|
| November  −5°C | February  −7°C |
| December  −8°C | March    −2°C |
| January    −9°C | April      +1°C |

Write the months in order from the one with the coldest average temperature to the one with the warmest.

Work Space:

Answer:

1. _____

2. _____

3. _____

4. _____

5. _____

6. _____

Name: _____

# Daily Word Problems

## WEEK 13 • DAY 5

**Vacations**

Krazy Planet Amusement Park is offering a 3-day pass that costs $65 per person. The Galaxy Five-Star Hotel next door to the park is offering a special rate of $170 per night.

1. Jolene's family of four will be buying 3-day passes as well as staying at the hotel for 2 nights. Fill in the blanks below to write a numerical expression that represents how much the family will pay for the passes and the hotel stay.

   (_____ × _____) + (_____ × _____)

2. Evaluate the expression you wrote above. How much will Jolene's family pay for the passes and the hotel?

   $_____

3. Jolene's parents plan to spend $\frac{1}{3}$ of their vacation money for the passes and the hotel. How much money did they save in total for their vacation?

   $_____

Name: _____

# Daily Word Problems

## WEEK 14 • DAY 1

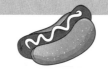

**Hot Dog Stand**

Corbin treated his two friends to Hamm's Hot Dogs, a popular local hot dog stand. He bought 2 regular hot dogs for $1.40 each, a large cheese dog for $1.80, and a large chili dog for $2.00.

1. How much did he pay for all the hot dogs?

2. What was the average price of one hot dog?

Work Space:

Answer:

1. $_____

2. $_____

---

Name: _____

# Daily Word Problems

## WEEK 14 • DAY 2

**Hot Dog Stand**

Mr. Hamm owns Hamm's Hot Dogs. Olivia made him a friendly challenge. If Olivia could eat 28 hot dogs in 8 minutes, she would get them free. If not, she would pay Mr. Hamm double the regular cost of the 28 hot dogs.

How many hot dogs per minute does Olivia need to eat to win the challenge? If the hot dogs usually cost $1.40 each, how much will Mr. Hamm receive if Olivia loses the challenge?

Work Space:

Answer:

_____ hot dogs per minute

$_____

# Daily Word Problems

**WEEK 14 • DAY 3**

**Hot Dog Stand**

Mr. Hamm doesn't want any hot dogs or buns left over at his hot dog stand at the end of each day. Hot dogs come in packages of 8. Buns come in packages of 10.

Mr. Hamm needs to prepare at least 180 hot dogs every day. What is the minimum number of packages of each that Mr. Hamm needs to buy in order to have the same number of hot dogs and buns?

**Work Space:**

**Answer:**

_____ packages of hot dogs

_____ packages of buns

---

# Daily Word Problems

**WEEK 14 • DAY 4**

**Hot Dog Stand**

Sofia had a coupon for 25% off her order. She bought a large hot dog, a medium drink, and a bag of pretzels. Their regular prices are shown below.

| | |
|---|---|
| large hot dog | $1.80 |
| medium drink | $1.50 |
| bag of pretzels | $1.30 |

How much did Sofia pay?

**Work Space:**

**Answer:**

$_____

# Daily Word Problems

## WEEK 14 • DAY 5

**Hot Dog Stand**

The graph shows the number of hot dogs Mr. Hamm has sold at his hot dog stand so far this week.

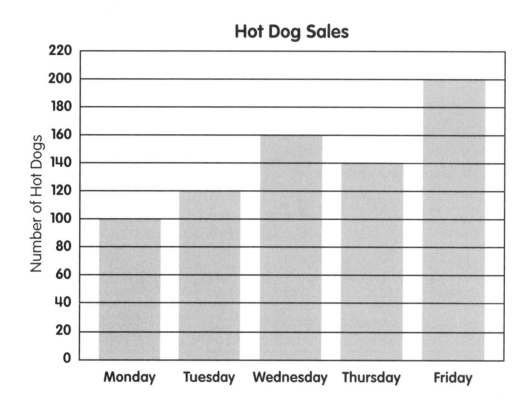

1. What was the total number of hot dogs sold? _____

2. What was the mean (average) number of hot dogs sold per day? _____

3. Suppose the hot dogs sold on Saturday increase the mean to 150. How many hot dogs would be sold on Saturday? Explain.

_____

_____

_____

_____

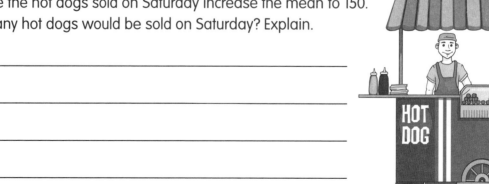

# Daily Word Problems

## WEEK 15 • DAY 1

**Hockey Math**

A hockey game has three 20-minute periods for a total playing time of 60 minutes. Average players play for about 22 minutes per game. The best players play for about 28 minutes per game.

About what percent of the total game time do average players play? What about the best players?

Work Space:

Answer:

average players:   about _____%

best players:   about _____%

---

# Daily Word Problems

## WEEK 15 • DAY 2

**Hockey Math**

A slapshot is a powerful shot a hockey player makes, much like a golf swing. With a slapshot, a puck reaches speeds of 100 miles per hour! A wrist shot is not as powerful or as fast, but the puck can still travel 80 miles per hour.

How many times faster does a puck travel with a slapshot than with a wrist shot?

Work Space:

Answer:

_____ times faster

# Daily Word Problems

**WEEK 15 • DAY 3**

**Hockey Math**

A goalie tries to stop a puck from entering the net. Each time the goalie stops a shot, it is called a "save." The number of saves divided by the total number of attempts to hit the puck into the net is the goalie's "save percentage."

Suppose there were 420 attempts and 378 saves by Roley the goalie. What would Roley's save percentage be?

Work Space:

Answer:

_____%

---

# Daily Word Problems

**WEEK 15 • DAY 4**

**Hockey Math**

A hockey goalie can touch the puck only when it is inside a certain area around the net. This area is in the shape of a trapezoid.

The net side of the trapezoid is 18 feet wide. The long side opposite the net is 28 feet wide. The distance between these sides is 11 feet. What is the area of the trapezoid?

Work Space:

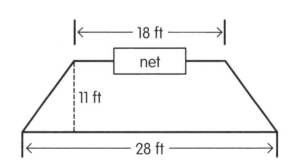

Answer:

_____ ft²

# Daily Word Problems

## WEEK 15 • DAY 5

**Hockey Math**

Hockey players are awarded "plus or minus numbers" when someone scores a goal. When a goal is scored, every player on the ice for the scoring team earns +1. Every player on the ice for the team that was scored against receives –1. The numbers for each player are tallied for each game and for the competitive season. Each player's tally is called a rating.

1. Annie and Skyler both play hockey on different teams. So far this season, Annie has a rating of +5. Skyler has a rating of –2. If Skyler is on the ice when her team scores its next 4 goals, will her rating be higher or lower than Annie's? Explain.

   _____

   _____

   _____

2. Evgeny plays hockey. He entered a game with a –3 rating. When the game was over, Evgeny's rating had changed to +1. What might have happened while Evgeny was on the ice? Give two possibilities.

   _____

   _____

   _____

   _____

   _____

   _____

Name: _____

## Daily Word Problems

**WEEK 16 • DAY 1**

**Trip to Canada**

Cam's family took a trip from his home in Utah to Canada. Cam discovered that a Canadian dollar not only looked different but also had a different value from the American dollar!

When Cam's parents exchanged $100 American dollars into Canadian dollars, they received $132.25. About how much was 1 American dollar worth in Canadian dollars that day?

Work Space:

Answer:

$_____

---

Name: _____

## Daily Word Problems

**WEEK 16 • DAY 2**

**Trip to Canada**

Cam's family traveled to Eastern Canada where public transportation is quite good. Even with the buses and trains they used to get around, though, Cam and his family walked an average of 12,543 steps a day to see the sights!

If their visit to Canada lasted 5 days, estimate how many steps they walked in all. Explain how you got your estimate.

Work Space:

Answer:

_____

_____

_____

_____

# Daily Word Problems

## WEEK 16 • DAY 3

**Trip to Canada**

Cam's family bought tickets to the Toronto Planetarium. The planetarium's show starts at 7:00 p.m.

It was an 11-minute walk from Cam's hotel to the subway station. The subway ride including the wait time would be 38 minutes. Cam and his family would then need 15 minutes to walk to the planetarium. What is the latest time they could leave the hotel to get to the planetarium by 7:00 p.m.?

Work Space:

Answer:

_____

---

# Daily Word Problems

## WEEK 16 • DAY 4

**Trip to Canada**

A Canadian doughnut shop had a special promotion while Cam and his family were on their trip. For every hot or cold drink a customer bought, the customer could purchase a set of 3 hockey cards for $1.

By the end of his trip, Cam had collected 39 hockey cards. If a drink cost at least $1.25, what is the minimum amount of money Cam had to spend to get his 39 hockey cards?

Work Space:

Answer:

$_____

# Daily Word Problems

## WEEK 16 • DAY 5

**Trip to Canada**

Cam had a simple map showing the location of his hotel and some nearby sights. Each square on the map represents one block.

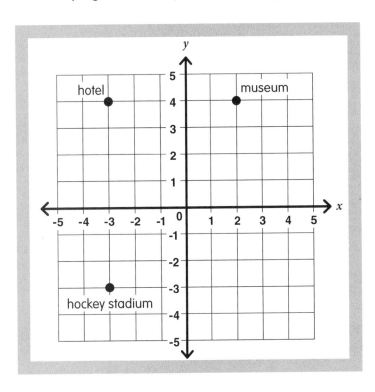

1. What are the coordinates of the hotel?            ( _____ , _____ )

2. What are the coordinates of the hockey stadium?            ( _____ , _____ )

3. What are the coordinates of the museum?            ( _____ , _____ )

   How many blocks is the museum from the hotel?            _____ blocks

4. Cam noticed that if he drew a line connecting the points representing the hockey stadium, hotel, museum, and aquarium, he'd make a rectangle.

   Draw the corresponding point on the map and label it *aquarium*.

   What are the coordinates of the aquarium?            ( _____ , _____ )

Name: _____

# Daily Word Problems

## WEEK 17 • DAY 1

**Gardening Time**

Kai's flower garden is in the shape of a parallelogram. Its area is 36 m². The garden's four side lengths are whole numbers.

1. What is the largest possible perimeter the garden could have? What would be its dimensions?

2. What is the smallest possible perimeter? What would be the garden's dimensions?

Work Space:

Answer:

1. largest perimeter: _____ m

   dimensions: _____ m × _____ m

2. smallest perimeter: _____ m

   dimensions: _____ m × _____ m

---

Name: _____

# Daily Word Problems

## WEEK 17 • DAY 2

**Gardening Time**

Mrs. O'Malley is designing a garden walkway that looks like this:

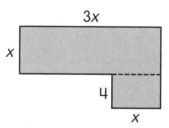

The area of the walkway is given by the expression $3x^2 + 4x$. What is the area if $x$ equals 5 feet?

Work Space:

Answer:

_____ ft²

# Daily Word Problems

**WEEK 17 • DAY 3**

**Gardening Time**

Work Space:

Mr. Chan built a rectangular planter frame. The outer dimensions are 10 ft × 8 ft × 2 ft. The walls are 6 in. thick.

1. What are the interior dimensions of the planter?

2. If he fills the planter $\frac{2}{3}$ full of soil, how much soil will he use?

6 in.

2 ft

8 ft

10 ft

Answer:

1. _____ ft × _____ ft × _____ ft

2. _____ ft³ of soil

---

# Daily Word Problems

**WEEK 17 • DAY 4**

**Gardening Time**

Work Space:

Tasha has a small garden in her yard. It is in the shape of a right triangle.

1. What is the perimeter of the garden? What is its area?

2. Tasha plans to make her garden larger by doubling all the side lengths. What will be the new perimeter and new area?

5 ft

3 ft

4 ft

Answer:

1. perimeter: _____ ft

   area: _____ ft²

2. new perimeter: _____ ft

   new area: _____ ft²

Name: _____

# Daily Word Problems
## WEEK 17 • DAY 5

**Gardening Time**

Ms. Bakshi works for the Grow-Right Garden Shop. Every month, she keeps track of the shop's income (the money earned) and expenses (the money spent).

Ms. Bakshi is working on the record sheet for last month. She records income as a positive number and expenses as a negative number. Use the memo, bill, and check below to fill in the rest of the record sheet. Then answer the questions.

| Item | Income | Expense |
|---|---|---|
| Sales: plants | | |
| Sales: tools/supplies | 6,035 | |
| Rent | | |
| Advertising | | |
| Purchase of new plants | | −3,200 |
| Utilities (water, electricity) | | −300 |
| Employee wages | | −4,000 |
| **Total** | | |

**Memo: total plant sales**

$7,380

---

**Daily News Ad Department Bill**

Fliers          $200.00
Display ad   $200.00

Total due     $400.00

---

**Grow-Right Garden Shop**          Date: 6/30/19

Property Guys                    $2,500

two thousand five hundred dollars

**Memo: July rent**          *Gini Bakshi*

1. What is the shop's total income?          $_____

2. What is the total amount of expenses?          $_____

3. What is the shop's profit (the money that is left after expenses have been deducted from the income)?          $_____

Name: _____

## Daily Word Problems

WEEK 18 • DAY 1

**Extreme Earth**

The lowest point on Earth is the Challenger Deep, an area in the Pacific Ocean. It is 36,070 feet below sea level. The highest elevation on Earth is Mount Everest. It rises 29,035 feet above sea level.

If Mount Everest were placed in the Challenger Deep, would water cover its peak? How far above or below sea level would the peak be?

Work Space:

Answer:

_____

_____

---

Name: _____

## Daily Word Problems

WEEK 18 • DAY 2

**Extreme Earth**

The Nile River in Africa is considered to be the longest river in the world. It is about 6,850 kilometers long. The Tamborasi River in Indonesia is one of the world's shortest rivers. It is only 20 meters long. That's shorter than the length of a soccer field!

How many times longer is the Nile River than the Tamborasi River?

Work Space:

Answer:

_____ times longer

Name: _____

# Daily Word Problems

## WEEK 18 • DAY 3

**Extreme Earth**

Mawsynram, a village in India, is the wettest place on Earth. It gets about 11,850 millimeters of rain per year!

1. About how many centimeters of rain fall in the village?

2. About how many inches of rain fall in the village?
   (Hint: One inch is about 2.54 centimeters.)

Work Space:

Answer:

1. about _____ centimeters

2. about _____ inches

---

Name: _____

# Daily Word Problems

## WEEK 18 • DAY 4

**Extreme Earth**

Iran's Lut Desert holds the record for having Earth's hottest surface temperature. Temperatures there can climb to a scorching 159°F! Antarctica holds the record for having the coldest temperature. Temperatures there can drop to a bone-chilling −136°F!

How many degrees Fahrenheit separate the two temperatures?

Work Space:

Answer:

_____ °F

## Daily Word Problems

**WEEK 18 • DAY 5**

**Extreme Earth**

Greenland's Jakobshavn Glacier is the world's fastest-moving glacier. It travels across land at speeds of up to 150 feet per day. When it reaches the coast, huge chunks of ice called bergs break off and float away in the ocean. (Researchers think this glacier is the source of the iceberg that hit the British ocean liner *Titanic* in 1912.)

1.  Suppose you wanted to find how far the glacier has traveled in a certain amount of time. Circle the expression you can use if *d* stands for the number of days. Then explain your choice.

    $150 + d$      $150/d$      $150d$      $150 - d$

    _____

    _____

    _____

2.  At its maximum speed, how many feet would the glacier travel in a year (365 days)? Use the expression you chose above to solve the problem.

    _____ feet

3.  About how many miles would the glacier travel in a year? (Hint: One mile equals 5,280 feet.)

    about _____ miles

Daily Word Problems • EMC 3096 • © Evan-Moor Corp.

## Daily Word Problems

**WEEK 19 • DAY 1**

**The Great Bike Race**

Name: _____

Juan is training for the Great Bike Race. Yesterday, Juan rode his bike for 45 minutes and covered 15 miles. He would like to increase his speed.

How many more miles would he need to ride in 45 minutes in order to reach his goal of 25 miles per hour?

Work Space:

Answer:

_____ more miles

## Daily Word Problems

**WEEK 19 • DAY 2**

**The Great Bike Race**

Name: _____

Kalani rode her bike every day to get ready for the Great Bike Race. The following numbers show how many miles she rode each day in one week:

12, 16, 13, 12, 15, 17, 20

How many miles did she average per day?

Work Space:

Answer:

_____ miles per day

Name: _____

## Daily Word Problems

**WEEK 19 • DAY 3**

**The Great Bike Race**

Work Space:

Each racer in the Great Bike Race competed on a 2-wheeled bike.

1. If *r* stands for the number of racers, what expression stands for the total number of wheels?

2. If there were 270 wheels in the race, how many racers were there? Write an equation and solve it.

Answer:

1. _____

2. _____

_____ racers

---

Name: _____

## Daily Word Problems

**WEEK 19 • DAY 4**

**The Great Bike Race**

Work Space:

The last racer in the Great Bike Race finished the race at 4:08 p.m. The range of completion times was 1 hour and 47 minutes.

Sid finished 6 minutes later than the first-place finisher. At what time did Sid cross the finish line?

Answer:

_____

 Daily Word Problems • EMC 3096 • © Evan-Moor Corp.

Name: _____

# Daily Word Problems

## WEEK 19 • DAY 5

**The Great Bike Race**

The histogram shows the range of ages of the racers who competed in the Great Bike Race.

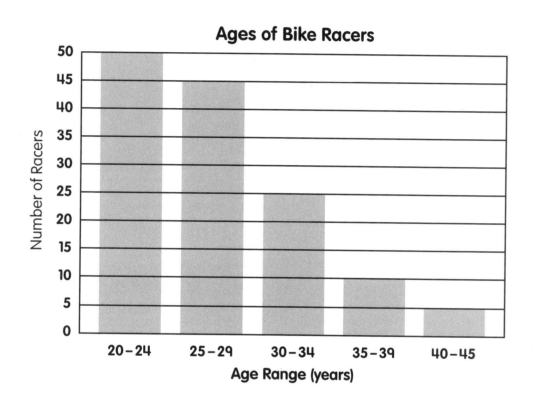

**Ages of Bike Racers**

Number of Racers / Age Range (years)

1. How many racers were there in all?                          _____ racers

2. How many racers were younger than 30?                  _____ racers

3. Describe the shape of the data distribution. (For example, are the data balanced, clustered, or spread out randomly?) What does this tell you about the racers' ages?

Name: _____

## Daily Word Problems

**WEEK 20 • DAY 1**

**Pancake Breakfast**

There are 40 tables set up at school for the annual pancake breakfast. Each table is 6 feet long and 2 feet wide. The students plan to cover each table with a paper tablecloth that extends an extra 3 inches over each edge.

What is the total area of the paper needed to cover all the tables? Express your answer in square feet.

Work Space:

Answer:

_____ square feet

---

Name: _____

## Daily Word Problems

**WEEK 20 • DAY 2**

**Pancake Breakfast**

A recipe for the pancake batter calls for $\frac{3}{4}$ cup of milk. The recipe serves 8 people.

The students want to make enough pancakes to serve 320 people. How many cups of milk will they need?

Work Space:

Answer:

_____ cups

# Daily Word Problems

**WEEK 20 • DAY 3**

**Pancake Breakfast**

Name: _____

Work Space:

Mr. Nimsky and Ms. Wu made pancakes at the pancake breakfast. Mr. Nimsky made stacks of 6 pancakes. Ms. Wu made stacks of 9. Later, they counted the pancakes in their stacks. They found they had made exactly the same number!

The number was more than 50 but less than 100. How many pancakes could Mr. Nimsky and Ms. Wu have made? Write three possibilities.

Answer:

_____, _____, _____

---

# Daily Word Problems

**WEEK 20 • DAY 4**

**Pancake Breakfast**

Name: _____

Work Space:

There were seven lines of people waiting to be served at the pancake breakfast. The lines had the following numbers of people in them:

48, 45, 42, 50, 41, 55, 39

What is the median for this set of data? (Hint: The median is the number in the center of the range.)

Answer:

_____ people

# Daily Word Problems

## WEEK 20 • DAY 5

**Pancake Breakfast**

The school principal brought 6 one-gallon jugs of syrup for the pancake breakfast. She decided to pour the syrup into bottles. She found enough bottles to put two on each of the 40 tables.

1. How many bottles were put on tables?

   _____ bottles

> 2 cups = 1 pint
>
> 2 pints = 1 quart
>
> 4 quarts = 1 gallon

2. The principal divided the syrup evenly into the bottles. How many cups of syrup did each bottle hold? Use the chart above to help you.

   _____ cups

3. Suppose one serving of syrup equaled $\frac{1}{4}$ cup. How many servings did the 6 gallons of syrup provide?

   _____ servings

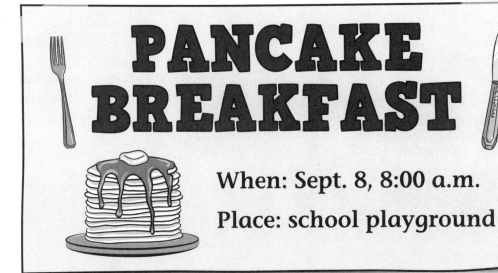

PANCAKE BREAKFAST

When: Sept. 8, 8:00 a.m.

Place: school playground

# Daily Word Problems

**WEEK 21 • DAY 1**

**Grub Club**

Zan and Gork are from the planet Yumm. They belong to the Grub Club, a group whose mission is to sample foods from around the galaxy.

Zan and Gork are visiting Australia, Earth. The first thing they did was to trade their alien money for Australian dollars. If they exchanged 750 Yumm dollars for 500 Australian dollars, how many Yumm dollars equaled one Australian dollar?

Work Space:

Answer:

_____ Yumm dollars

---

# Daily Word Problems

**WEEK 21 • DAY 2**

**Grub Club**

Zan and Gork heard about tacos and set aside $25 to try them. They found a taco stand that sells tacos for $1.25 and a diner that sells them for $2.50.

1. Use the inequality $1.25t \leq 25$ to find the maximum number of tacos they can order from the taco stand.

2. Write and solve an inequality to find the maximum number of tacos they can order from the diner.

Work Space:

Answer:

1. _____ tacos

2. _____

_____ tacos

**Grub Club**

# Daily Word Problems

## WEEK 21 • DAY 3

Name: _____

Zan and Gork ate at a restaurant named Veggie Temptations. They shared a zucchini boat filled with tomatoes, onions, and peppers for $40 and a dish of stuffed mushrooms for $25. Everything was super tasty! They got ready to pay their bill.

After a helpful customer told them about tipping, Zan and Gork added money for a 20% tip. How much did they pay for their meal?

Work Space:

Answer:

$_____

---

**Grub Club**

# Daily Word Problems

## WEEK 21 • DAY 4

Name: _____

Zan and Gork found a take-out place that served Caramel Cricket Cake. Zan ordered a slice to eat on the spaceship.

The cake came in a container that was shaped like a triangular prism. The diagram shows its dimensions. What was the surface area of the container?

10 in.
6 in.
8 in.
8 in.

Work Space:

Answer:

_____ in.²

Name: _____

# Daily Word Problems
## WEEK 21 • DAY 5

**Grub Club**

Zan and Gork got this message from the leader of the Grub Club:

Dear Zan and Gork,
I hope you're enjoying your tasty visit to Planet Earth. Here are the coordinates of some restaurants we want you to try:

Fresh Farm Fare (–4, 3)     Sizzling Supper (–6, –5)
Weirdly Wonderful (4, 2)     Zeal for Meals (2, –6)

Come home soon and give us a full account of your earthly meals. We eagerly await your report.

Meelo,
Grub Club President

1. Plot the points on the grid. Label each one with the first letter of the matching restaurant. Then write the quadrant where each point is located—I, II, III, or IV.

**F** quadrant _____     **S** quadrant _____

**W** quadrant _____     **Z** quadrant _____

2. Zan and Gork discovered a restaurant named Out of This World. To find its location, reflect point **W** across the *x*-axis. Plot the point on the grid and label it **O**.

What are its coordinates?

_____

In which quadrant is point **O** located?

quadrant _____

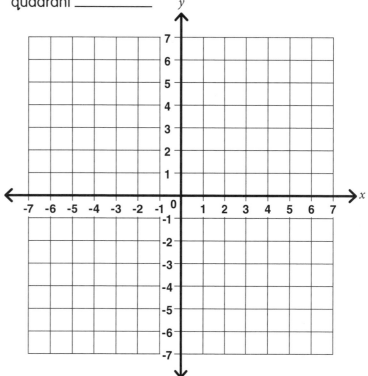

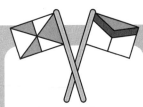

Name: _____

# Daily Word Problems

## WEEK 22 • DAY 1

 **Flag Designs**

Germaine designed a flag in art class. It looks like this:

$3\frac{1}{2}$ in.   $8\frac{1}{2}$ in.

8 in.

$8\frac{1}{2}$ in.   $3\frac{1}{2}$ in.

What is the area of the black stripe in the middle of the flag?

Work Space:

Answer:

_____ in.$^2$

---

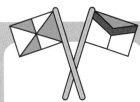

Name: _____

# Daily Word Problems

## WEEK 22 • DAY 2

**Flag Designs**

Ratna designed this flag:

20 cm

12 cm   12 cm

What is the area of the gray triangle in the middle of the flag?

Work Space:

Answer:

_____ cm$^2$

Daily Word Problems • EMC 3096 • © Evan-Moor Corp.

Name: _____

# Daily Word Problems

## WEEK 22 • DAY 3

**Flag Designs**

Jazmin sewed a flag using small squares of fabric. The squares were red, yellow, and blue. The ratio of red squares to yellow squares was 1:2. The ratio of red squares to blue squares was 1:3.

There were 18 squares in all. How many were there of each color?

Work Space:

Answer:

red _____

yellow _____

blue _____

Name: _____

# Daily Word Problems

## WEEK 22 • DAY 4

**Flag Designs**

Matthew is making colorful flags to sell at a crafts fair. He wants to make at least 20 flags. So far he has made 8 flags.

Write and solve an inequality to find the smallest number of flags Matthew still needs to make.

Work Space:

Answer:

_____

_____ more flags

Name: _____

# Daily Word Problems

## WEEK 22 • DAY 5

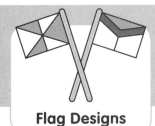

Cody designs flags that are rectangular. Jodie designs flags that are triangular. Before they make their flags, they sketch them on one-inch graph paper.

1. Cody designed a flag that was 6 in. wide and 4 in. tall. It is shown at the right. Jodie designed a flag that had the same area as Cody's flag, but it was in the shape of a right triangle.

   Draw a possible shape for Jodie's flag on the grid. What are its base and height?

   base _____ in.

   height _____ in.

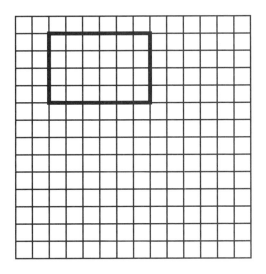

2. Last week, Jodie designed the flag on the right. It is in the shape of an isosceles triangle. Cody designed a flag last week, too. It had the same area as Jodie's flag.

   Draw a possible shape for Cody's flag. What are its base and height?

   base _____ in.

   height _____ in.

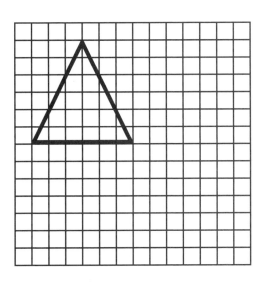

# Daily Word Problems

## WEEK 23 • DAY 1

**Dog Salon**

Name: _____

Work Space:

There are 15 groomers who work at Furry Clips Dog Salon. They put all the tips they earn into a bowl and divide the money equally at the end of each week.

Last week, the money in the bowl totaled $2,040. How much money did each person receive in tips?

Answer:

$_____

---

# Daily Word Problems

## WEEK 23 • DAY 2

**Dog Salon**

Name: _____

Work Space:

Belen is the owner of Petite Paws Palace, a salon for small dogs. Last week, she offered a special low rate for a shampoo and got a lot of extra business.

During the first three days, Belen earned $72, $96, and $104 just from shampoo sales. What is the maximum amount she could have charged for that service?

Answer:

$_____

# Daily Word Problems

## WEEK 23 • DAY 3

**Dog Salon**

Fifi the poodle got a bubble bath and a stylish haircut. Mrs. Barker, her owner, was so pleased that she gave the dog groomer a 25% tip.

The bath and cut cost $64. How much did Mrs. Barker pay in total?

**Work Space:**

**Answer:**

$_____

# Daily Word Problems

## WEEK 23 • DAY 4

**Dog Salon**

Danilo budgeted $210 for his dog's grooming this year. His groomer charges $35 per visit.

1. If $g$ stands for the number of grooming visits, which expression shows how much they will cost?

$35 + g$    $35g$    $35 - g$    $g \div 35$

2. Write and solve an inequality for the maximum number of grooming visits Danilo's dog can have this year.

**Work Space:**

**Answer:**

1. _____

2. _____

_____ grooming visits

Name: _____

# Daily Word Problems
## WEEK 23 • DAY 5

**Dog Salon**

Yuna has a lot of choices when she needs to take her dog for a bath and trim. That's because there are three dog salons in her neighborhood!

The star on the map shows the location of Yuna's house. Each square stands for one block. Use the coordinates to locate the salons on the map. Then draw the points and label them.

Awesome Paws **A** (5, −5)

Bow-wow Spa **B** (−4, −5)

Canine Clips **C** (5, 2)

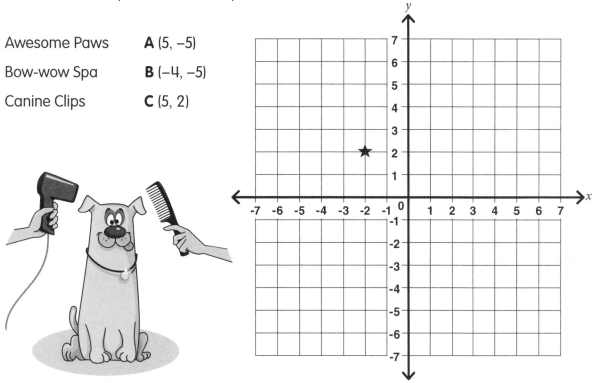

1. How far away is Awesome Paws from the Bow-wow Spa?    _____ blocks

2. How many blocks away is Canine Clips from Awesome Paws?    _____ blocks

3. What coordinates show where Yuna lives?    _____

4. Which dog salon is closest to Yuna's house?    _____

    How many blocks away is it? (Count the blocks by moving only horizontally or vertically on the map.)    _____ blocks

# Daily Word Problems

## WEEK 24 • DAY 1

**Vending Machines**

Sid noticed that his school got a vending machine full of healthy snacks. Sid measured the machine. He found that it is 6 ft high, 3 ft wide, and $2\frac{1}{2}$ ft deep.

What is the volume of the vending machine? What is its surface area?

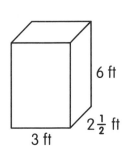

6 ft

$2\frac{1}{2}$ ft

3 ft

Work Space:

Answer:

volume: _____ ft³

surface area: _____ ft²

---

# Daily Word Problems

## WEEK 24 • DAY 2

**Vending Machines**

A vending machine had bottles of water for $1.25 and apple juice boxes for $1.75.

1. Let *w* stand for the number of water bottles and *a* for the number of apple juice boxes. What would 1.25*w* and 1.75*a* represent?

2. Write an expression that shows the total cost of 3 bottles of water and 2 boxes of apple juice. Then evaluate the expression.

Work Space:

Answer:

1. 1.25*w*: _____

   _____

   1.75*a*: _____

   _____

2. _____

   Total cost: $_____

# Daily Word Problems

## WEEK 24 • DAY 3

**Vending Machines**

Name: _____

Luc was at the airport waiting to board the plane. Suddenly, he realized he had packed jeans but no T-shirts. Luckily, there was a vending machine nearby stocked with T-shirts. Each one cost $16. Luc had $80 in his wallet.

Let *s* equal the number of T-shirts. Write and solve an inequality showing the maximum number of T-shirts Luc can buy.

Work Space:

Answer:

_____

maximum number of T-shirts: _____

---

# Daily Word Problems

## WEEK 24 • DAY 4

**Vending Machines**

Name: _____

Sven owns 10 vending machines. Every day, he drives out to check them and restock items. Sven calculates the distance he drives by using the expression $r \times t$, where *r* is the average speed of his car (in miles per hour) and *t* is the amount of driving time.

One day, Sven determined that he drove 40 miles per hour for 4.5 hours. How far did Sven drive?

Work Space:

Answer:

_____ miles

# Daily Word Problems

## WEEK 24 • DAY 5

**Vending Machines**

A cupcake company decided to try using vending machines to sell its cupcakes. Ms. Sweets, the company president, decided to test customers' responses by setting up a machine in a mall.

1. Ms. Sweets was pleasantly surprised. People loved the idea of a cupcake vending machine. During the test period, customers bought 800 cupcakes a day from the machine!

   How many cupcakes a week was that?

   _____ cupcakes

2. Each cupcake in the machine cost $3.25. If 800 cupcakes a day were sold, how much money did the vending machine bring in every week?

   $_____

3. Ms. Sweets decided to buy 3 additional vending machines. If they turn out to be as popular as the first machine, how many dollars a month (30 days) can Ms. Sweets expect from all vending machine sales?

   $_____

# Daily Word Problems

## WEEK 25 · DAY 1

**Mr. Topper's Toys**

Mr. Topper is a toymaker. He made a sailboat that has a sail in the shape of a right triangle.

The area of the sail is 48 square centimeters. What could its base and height be? (Use only whole numbers for the dimensions.)

Work Space:

Answer:

base: _____ centimeters

height: _____ centimeters

---

# Daily Word Problems

## WEEK 25 · DAY 2

**Mr. Topper's Toys**

Mr. Topper made a toy car that he modeled after his own car. The toy car is $\frac{1}{20}$ the length of the actual car.

If Mr. Topper's car is 150 inches long, how long is the toy car?

Work Space:

Answer:

_____ inches

# Daily Word Problems

## WEEK 25 • DAY 3

**Mr. Topper's Toys**

Mr. Topper enjoys carving toy animals out of wood. All of his figures are either farm animals or forest animals. For every 2 farm animals he makes, Mr. Topper makes 3 forest animals.

Last month, Mr. Topper carved 15 toy animals. How many were farm animals, and how many were forest animals?

Work Space:

Answer:

_____ farm animals

_____ forest animals

---

# Daily Word Problems

## WEEK 25 • DAY 4

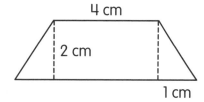

**Mr. Topper's Toys**

Mr. Topper built some furniture for a dollhouse he made. Yesterday, he made a table that was in the shape of a trapezoid. The top of the table looked like this:

4 cm

2 cm

1 cm

What was the area of the tabletop?

Work Space:

Answer:

_____ cm²

# Daily Word Problems

## WEEK 25 • DAY 5

**Mr. Topper's Toys**

Mr. Topper just finished making a set of wooden blocks.
The blocks come in these three sizes:

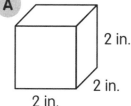

A — 2 in. / 2 in. / 2 in.

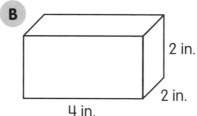

B — 2 in. / 2 in. / 4 in.

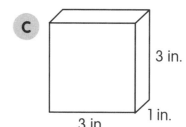

C — 3 in. / 3 in. / 1 in.

1. What is the surface area of each block?

   A _____ in.²

   B _____ in.²

   C _____ in.²

2. Mr. Topper made 20 blocks of each size.
   What is the total surface area of all the blocks?

   _____ in.²

3. Mr. Topper is going to paint all the blocks. If one bottle
   of paint covers 10 square feet, how many bottles of paint
   will he need for all the blocks? (Hint: You will need to find
   how many square inches equals 1 square foot.)

   _____ bottles of paint

# Daily Word Problems

## WEEK 26 • DAY 1

**Wildlife Animal Park**

Lena and her class are going on a field trip to a wildlife animal park. The regular price for admission is $35 for adults and $20 for students. Lena's school will get a 15% discount for having more than 30 people in the group.

With 4 adults and 32 students in the group, how much will their admission fee cost?

**Work Space:**

Answer:

$_____

---

# Daily Word Problems

## WEEK 26 • DAY 2

**Wildlife Animal Park**

The wildlife animal park is home to 7 elephants. Their ages in years are as follows:

30, 19, 35, 25, 16, 37, 20

1. What is the median age of the group?

2. What is the mean age of the group?

**Work Space:**

Answer:

1. _____ years old

2. _____ years old

Name: _____

# Daily Word Problems

**WEEK 26 • DAY 3**

**Wildlife Animal Park**

A group of 60 students was visiting the Critter Corral petting area. Three-fifths of the group bought bags of food for the animals at $1.75 each.

1. How many students bought bags of food?

2. How much did they spend in total?

Work Space:

Answer:

1. _____ students

2. $_____

---

Name: _____

# Daily Word Problems

**WEEK 26 • DAY 4**

**Wildlife Animal Park**

Perky, one of the penguins that lives at Penguin Palace, loves to swim and dive. Yesterday, the penguin climbed to the top of a 25-ft ledge. Then he jumped off the ledge and dove to a depth of –156 ft!

What was the total length of Perky's dive?

Work Space:

Answer:

_____ ft

# Daily Word Problems

## WEEK 26 • DAY 5

**Wildlife Animal Park**

The Lion Country enclosure at a wildlife animal park forms a hexagonal shape.

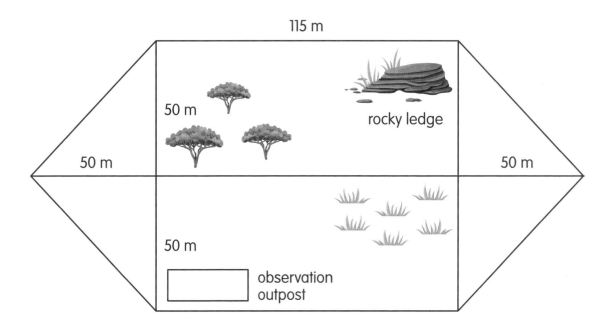

115 m

50 m

50 m

50 m

rocky ledge

50 m

50 m

observation outpost

1. What is the total area of the enclosure?

   _____ m²

2. The area of a football field measures about 5,350 square meters. Is the area of Lion Country greater than or less than the area of a football field?

   By how many square meters is it greater or less?

   _____

   _____

Name: _____

## Daily Word Problems

**Game Night**

### WEEK 27 • DAY 1

Gladtown School hosted Game Night for students and their families. A total of 240 people attended.

There were 16 tables set up in the school cafeteria for the event. Every table had the same number of people. How many people sat at each table?

Work Space:

Answer:

_____ people

---

Name: _____

## Daily Word Problems

**Game Night**

### WEEK 27 • DAY 2

Ramon, Cheri, and Aiden played a game in which they earned or lost points. Here are their results after the first round:

Ramon: −1     Cheri: −8     Aiden: −3

1. Who had the highest score?

2. Who had the lowest score?

3. Was the middle score closer to the highest score or the lowest score? Explain.

Work Space:

Answer:

1. _____

2. _____

3. _____

_____

_____

## Daily Word Problems

**WEEK 27 • DAY 3**

**Game Night**

Ben and his family worked on a 3-dimensional pyramid puzzle. They first finished putting the 6-inch square base together. Then they started piecing together the 4 triangular faces.

Each triangle had a base of 6 inches and a height of 8 inches. What will be the surface area of the completed pyramid puzzle?

Work Space:

Answer:

_____ in.$^2$

---

## Daily Word Problems

**WEEK 27 • DAY 4**

**Game Night**

Nadja and her family played a board game in which the loser has to divide his or her points equally among the other players. Poor Nadja! She lost the first round and had to divide 2,345 points among 5 players.

How many points did each player receive?

Work Space:

Answer:

_____ points

Name: _____

# Daily Word Problems

## WEEK 27 • DAY 5

**Game Night**

Gladtown School's Game Night was a huge success! There were 240 people who attended, and everyone had a great time.

The circle graph shows the types of games that were played and the percent of people who played them.

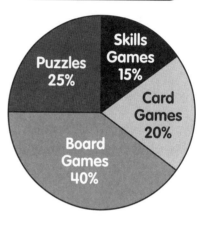

**Game Selections**

Puzzles 25%
Skills Games 15%
Card Games 20%
Board Games 40%

1. How many people played card games?

_____ people

2. What kind of game was the most popular?

_____

How many people played these games?

_____ people

3. How many more people worked on puzzles than played skills games such as beanbag toss?

_____ more people

4. If 6 people who worked on puzzles had played card games instead, how would those percents have been affected?

_____

_____

Name: _____

# Daily Word Problems

## WEEK 28 • DAY 1

**Sherman's Shapes**

Sherman creates interesting shapes with tiles. He draws his ideas on paper first so he can see what the tiles will look like. Here is one of his drawings:

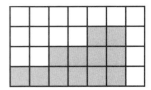

What is the perimeter of the shaded shape? What is the area?

Work Space:

Answer:

perimeter: _____ units

area: _____ square units

---

Name: _____

# Daily Word Problems

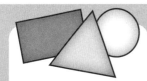

## WEEK 28 • DAY 2

**Sherman's Shapes**

Sherman had an idea for a tile design. He started by drawing a quadrilateral on a coordinate plane. The coordinates of the vertices were (–1, 2), (3, 2), (–3, –2), and (1, –2).

1. What kind of quadrilateral did Sherman make?

2. What is its area?

Work Space:

Draw Sherman's quadrilateral.

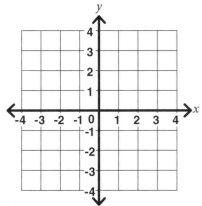

Answer:

1. _____

2. _____ square units

# Daily Word Problems

**WEEK 28 • DAY 3**

**Sherman's Shapes**

Sherman made this figure by overlapping two same-sized squares:

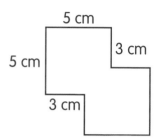

5 cm

5 cm

3 cm

3 cm

What is the area of the figure?
Explain how you solved the problem.

Work Space:

Answer:

area: _____ cm²

_____

_____

_____

_____

_____

---

# Daily Word Problems

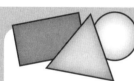

**WEEK 28 • DAY 4**

**Sherman's Shapes**

Sherman designed a shape that looked like this:

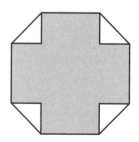

How many lines of symmetry does it have?

Work Space:

Draw the lines of symmetry on the shape.

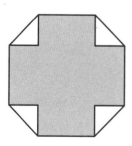

Answer:

_____ lines of symmetry

# Daily Word Problems

## WEEK 28 • DAY 5

**Sherman's Shapes**

Sherman arranged 1-inch square tiles to make a larger square with an interesting design.

Each tile looked like this:

Sherman's large square looked like this:

What is the minimum number of tiles Sherman used to make the large square?                                              _____ tiles

Test your answer by using the grid below to re-create Sherman's shape. You don't have to use the entire grid

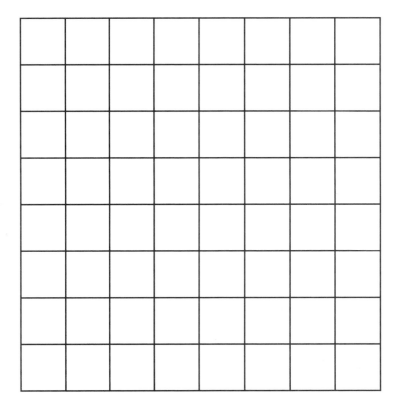

## Daily Word Problems

**WEEK 29 • DAY 1**

**Hiking Fun**

Ruben and Monique are getting their backpacks ready for a hiking trip. They know their packs should not weigh more than 20% of their body weight. Ruben weighs 110 pounds and Monique weighs 95 pounds.

What is the maximum combined weights of their backpacks?

Work Space:

Answer:

_____ pounds

---

## Daily Word Problems

**Hiking Fun**

**WEEK 29 • DAY 2**

Nevine and her parents were hiking in the Andes. They came to a bridge that had a weight limit of 500 kg. Nevine's father weighs 82 kg, her mother weighs 61 kg, and Nevine weighs 39 kg.

If Nevine's family crossed the bridge at the same time, how much additional weight could the bridge hold? Write an inequality to solve the problem. Use *w* for the unknown weight.

Work Space:

Answer:

inequality: _____

_____ additional kg

# Daily Word Problems

**WEEK 29 • DAY 3**

**Hiking Fun**

Keanu went on a hike. He started out with a full bottle of water. Every half hour, he sipped $\frac{1}{4}$ of the water that was left in his bottle.

1. After half an hour, how full was the bottle?

2. After an hour, how full was the bottle?

Work Space:

Answer:

1. _____ full

2. _____ full

---

# Daily Word Problems

**WEEK 29 • DAY 4**

**Hiking Fun**

Sam and his hiking club went on a 2-hour hike. They started the hike at an elevation of 1,850 meters and kept a log of the changes in elevation every 20 minutes. Here are the entries in their logbook:

+46, +61, −6, +40, −5, +30

What was the elevation at the end of their hike?

Work Space:

Answer:

_____ meters

Name: _____

# Daily Word Problems

## WEEK 29 • DAY 5

**Hiking Fun**

The following list shows the number of hours it took 10 hikers to climb to the top of Bluetop Peak:

| | | | | |
|---|---|---|---|---|
| 2 | $1\frac{1}{2}$ | 2 | $2\frac{3}{4}$ | $2\frac{1}{2}$ |
| $2\frac{1}{2}$ | $2\frac{3}{4}$ | $2\frac{1}{4}$ | 2 | $2\frac{1}{4}$ |

1. Make a line plot of the data. The first entry has been plotted for you.

### Time Taken to Reach Bluetop Peak

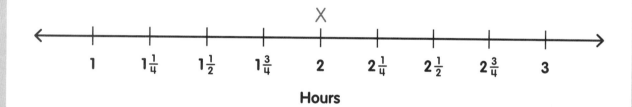

**Hours**

2. Find the mean, median, and mode of the data set.

   mean _____     median _____     mode _____

3. Suppose one more hiker's time of 3 hours was added to the data set. How would this affect the mean, median, and mode?

   _____

   _____

   _____

   _____

Name: _____

# Daily Word Problems

## WEEK 30 • DAY 1

The **Great Detective**

Detective Dev was investigating a theft at an art gallery. He saw that from a wall of 50 paintings, pieces 2, 3, 5, 7, 11, 13, 17, and 19 were taken. He knew the thieves would be back for more. Sure enough, he caught them in the act the next night!

Dev had noticed a number pattern. Which paintings were the thieves planning to take the second night? How do you know?

Work Space:

Answer:

paintings _____

_____

_____

_____

---

Name: _____

# Daily Word Problems

## WEEK 30 • DAY 2

The **Great Detective**

Three witnesses reported damage to a sculpture entitled "Cubes" in the park.

- Ana: "The vandal smashed the tall cube on the left!"
- Bob: "No, it's the cube on the right."
- Cil: "The middle cube was hit."
- Ana and Bob: "Middle? There are only 2 columns of cubes!"

Detective Dev figured out they had been looking from different places. Where was each witness located?

Work Space:

Answer:

Ana: _____

Bob: _____

Cil: _____

# Daily Word Problems

## WEEK 30 • DAY 3

The **Great Detective**

On Sunday, April 1, 2018, a burglar bagged an earring made of a rare gem called painite and left this note:

> *Beware! I will be back to take this earring's mate the next time April 1 falls on the same day of the week!*

Most years have 365 days. Leap years, which are multiples of 4, have 366 days. Dev said, "We'll be ready to bungle that burglary!" On April 1 of what year will Dev catch the criminal?

**Work Space:**

**Answer:**

the year _____

---

# Daily Word Problems

## WEEK 30 • DAY 4

The **Great Detective**

Gina called Detective Dev in a panic. "I'm house-sitting. My neighbor left me $70 in cash to make some payments. A calendar from a fundraiser will be delivered. I need to pay twice the cost of the calendar to the gardener. Then I have to give Ms. Taban 4 times the calendar cost for cleaning the gutters!"

"Don't worry," said Dev. "I know how much each person should receive!" What are the payment amounts?

**Work Space:**

**Answer:**

calendar     $_____

gardener     $_____

Ms. Taban   $_____

# Daily Word Problems

## WEEK 30 · DAY 5

**The Great Detective**

Detective Dev knows the five thieves who stole from the Forever-After Fairy Tale Museum. Read the clues and fill in the chart to determine what each thief stole. When you know that a name and an item **don't** go together, make an **X** under that item and across from that name. When you know that a name and an item **do** go together, write **YES** in that box.

**Clues:**

- Zappo did not get the slipper or the crown.
- Bugsy got the egg or the seeds.
- Sneakers and Curly did not get the mirror or the egg.
- Shifty and Curly did not get the crown or the seeds.
- Zappo got something that could be planted.

| | golden egg | glass slipper | enchanted mirror | jeweled crown | magic bean seeds |
|---|---|---|---|---|---|
| **Bugsy** | | | | | |
| **Curly** | | | | | |
| **Zappo** | | | | | |
| **Shifty** | | | | | |
| **Sneakers** | | | | | |

Write the name of each thief beside the item he or she stole.

golden egg _____    jeweled crown _____

glass slipper _____    magic bean seeds _____

enchanted mirror _____

# Daily Word Problems

## WEEK 31 • DAY 1

**Fish Tales**

Anoosh loves to go fishing with his dad and mom. One day, his mom caught a fish that weighed 3 lb 2 oz. His dad's fish weighed 7 oz less than his mom's fish. Anoosh caught a fish that weighed twice as much as his dad's fish.

How much did Anoosh's fish weigh? (Hint: 16 oz = 1 lb)

Work Space:

Answer:

_____ lb _____ oz

---

# Daily Word Problems

## WEEK 31 • DAY 2

**Fish Tales**

Lani went fishing with her dad. She caught a fish that was 19 inches less than twice the length of her dad's fish. Her dad's fish was $\frac{2}{3}$ yard in length.

How many inches long was Lani's fish?

Work Space:

Answer:

_____ inches

Name: _____

# Daily Word Problems

**WEEK 31 • DAY 3**

**Fish Tales**

Shayna and her family went fishing. They put their minnows in a rectangular container that was 12 cm × 12 cm × 20 cm.

What was the volume of the container? What was its surface area?

Work Space:

Answer:

volume: _____ cm$^3$

surface area: _____ cm$^2$

---

Name: _____

# Daily Word Problems

**WEEK 31 • DAY 4**

**Fish Tales**

A lake was stocked regularly with catfish and trout. There was a limit on how many fish a person could catch daily. The daily catfish limit was 3, and the daily trout limit was 5.

Suppose a person caught the maximum daily limit every day. If the person caught a total of 56 fish, how many catfish and how many trout were caught?

Work Space:

Answer:

_____ catfish

_____ trout

# Daily Word Problems

## WEEK 31 • DAY 5

**Fish Tales**

The box plot shows the ages of people who went fishing at a lake one weekend.

**Ages of People Who Went Fishing**

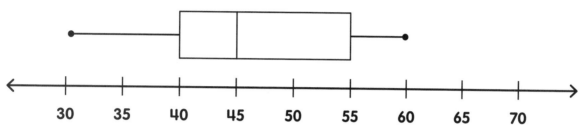

1. What is the median of the data set? _____

2. What is the range? _____

3. The first quartile and third quartile tell you where the middle 50% of the data lie. What are the first quartile and third quartile?

   first quartile _____     third quartile _____

4. What is the interquartile range? _____

5. The line representing the median is not in the middle of the box. What does this tell you about the ages of the people who went fishing?

   _____

   _____

Name: _____

# Daily Word Problems

**WEEK 32 • DAY 1**

**At the Movies**

Vera, Reina, and Elena plan to see the latest sci-fi thriller *Teacher from Planet X*. If they go to a Saturday night showing, the tickets will cost $15.00 each. If they go on Saturday morning, the tickets will be $12.50 each.

The girls have a 20% off coupon for evening admission. Which showing is the better buy? Explain.

Work Space:

Answer:

_____

_____

_____

_____

---

Name: _____

# Daily Word Problems

**WEEK 32 • DAY 2**

**At the Movies**

*Teacher from Planet X* was so popular that fans lined up early on opening day. Jian and Josh arrived 6 hours before the theater doors opened in order to buy tickets and get good seats. Then they sat through a half hour of commercials and 15 minutes of previews. When the movie started, they sat glued to their seats for 2 hours and 15 minutes. How much time in all did they spend at the theater?

Work Space:

Answer:

_____

Daily Word Problems • EMC 3096 • © Evan-Moor Corp.

# Daily Word Problems

**WEEK 32 • DAY 3**

**At the Movies**

Name: _____

The Galaxy Cinema has 400 seats. When Akua and her parents and little brother arrived, 45% of the seats were already filled.

1. How many empty seats were there when Akua's family first got to the theater?

2. After Akua's family sat down in the theater, what percent of seats were then filled?

Work Space:

Answer:

1. _____ empty seats

2. _____%

---

Name: _____

# Daily Word Problems

**WEEK 32 • DAY 4**

**At the Movies**

Great Times Theater had six showings of the movie *Invisible Hero* last Saturday. The attendance at five of the showings was 240, 275, 250, 300, and 290.

If the mean attendance was 275, how many people attended the sixth showing?

Work Space:

Answer:

_____ people

# Daily Word Problems

## WEEK 32 • DAY 5

**At the Movies**

The following list shows the running times of six blockbuster movies:

| | |
|---|---|
| *Teacher from Planet X* | 133 minutes |
| *Star Battle* | 147 minutes |
| *Invisible Hero* | 118 minutes |
| *Ant Guy Meets Bee Girl* | 129 minutes |
| *Bella and the Bubble Gum Factory* | 115 minutes |
| *Spy Guy to the Rescue* | 140 minutes |

1. Find the following measures of variation for the data.

    median _____

    range _____

    first quartile _____

    third quartile _____

    interquartile range _____

2. What is the approximate mean running time?

    _____ minutes

## Daily Word Problems

**Six-Hand Sam**

**WEEK 33 • DAY 1**

**Silly Stories**

Name: _____

Mr. Ozawa was driving to work when he saw a gorilla at the side of the road. The gorilla was holding a large diamond-shaped kite.

"Can you give me a lift to the park?" asked the gorilla.

"Sure, get in!" said Mr. Ozawa. The gorilla fit in the car but the kite barely did. It measured 2 ft across and 4 ft from top to bottom. What was the area of the kite?

Work Space:

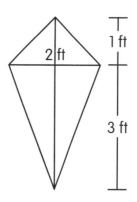

Answer:

_____ ft²

---

## Daily Word Problems

**Six-Hand Sam**

**WEEK 33 • DAY 2**

**Silly Stories**

Name: _____

Duchess Dilly collects shoes. In fact, she has two closets full of just shoes! One day she said, "Oh dear! I have 3 times as many shoes in Closet A as I do in Closet B. I had better fix that!"

Duchess Dilly moved 60 shoes from Closet A to Closet B. Once she did that, each closet had the same number of shoes. How many shoes were in each closet to start? How many were in each closet at the end?

Work Space:

Answer:

Closet A had _____ shoes to start.

Closet B had _____ shoes to start.

Each closet had _____ shoes at the end.

© Evan-Moor Corp. • EMC 3096 • *Daily Word Problems*

**107**

## Daily Word Problems

**WEEK 33 • DAY 3**

**Silly Stories**

Name: _____

A basset hound and a beagle had a contest. They wanted to see who could bury bones the fastest.

The basset hound buried 6 bones in 24 minutes. The beagle buried 15 bones in 45 minutes.

Which dog was faster? How do you know?

Work Space:

Answer:

The _____ was faster.

_____

_____

_____

_____

---

## Daily Word Problems

**WEEK 33 • DAY 4**

**Silly Stories**

Name: _____

Two polar bears, Crystal and Flake, were knitting warm sweaters for their friends. Crystal knitted $\frac{3}{4}$ as many sweaters as Flake. They knitted 63 sweaters in all.

How many sweaters did each polar bear knit?

Work Space:

Answer:

Crystal: _____ sweaters

Flake: _____ sweaters

# Daily Word Problems

## WEEK 33 • DAY 5

**Silly Stories**

Rusty Rabbit planted a rectangular garden full of carrots. The garden was 8 feet long and 6 feet wide. Rusty wanted to protect his carrots from his nosy neighbor, Henry Horse, so he built a fence around the entire garden. The fence stood $\frac{1}{2}$ ft away from the edge of the garden.

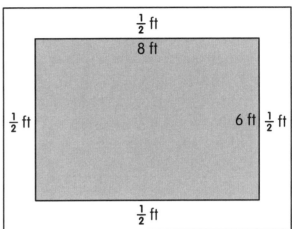

1. What were the dimensions of the fence?

   _____ ft long, _____ ft wide

2. What was the total area of the space inside the fence?    _____ ft²

3. What was the area of the garden only?    _____ ft²

4. What was the area of the space that was between the garden and the fence?    _____ ft²

   Explain how you solved the problem.

   _____

   _____

Name: _____

# Daily Word Problems

## WEEK 34 • DAY 1

**School Fundraising**

Jacob's school held a crafts fair to raise money for field trips. Jacob had $50 to spend. He spent $12.50 on a hand-carved airplane.

Jacob was so happy with his airplane that he wanted to buy a second item. What is the maximum amount he could spend? Write an inequality to solve the problem. Use *p* to stand for the unknown amount.

Work Space:

Answer:

inequality: _____

$_____

Name: _____

# Daily Word Problems

## WEEK 34 • DAY 2

**School Fundraising**

The students at Grover School want to raise money for some new playground equipment. A swing set costs $350, and a climbing set costs 5 times more than that.

If the students have collected $\frac{2}{3}$ of the total cost, how much more money do they need to raise?

Work Space:

Answer:

$_____ more

Daily Word Problems • EMC 3096 • © Evan-Moor Corp.

Name: _____

# Daily Word Problems

**WEEK 34 • DAY 3**

**School Fundraising**

Ms. Esparza's class held a garage sale to raise money for sports equipment. There were 2,625 baseball cards donated for the sale.

Twenty-five people got together to buy all the cards. If they divided the cards equally among themselves, how many cards did each person get?

Work Space:

Answer:

_____ cards

---

Name: _____

# Daily Word Problems

**WEEK 34 • DAY 4**

**School Fundraising**

The students in Mr. Park's class will sell magazine subscriptions to raise money for their school. The statistics from the magazine company show that 2 out of every 5 people who are asked will buy a subscription from a student.

According to the company's statistics, how many subscriptions can Emi expect to sell if she asks 145 people?

Work Space:

Answer:

_____ subscriptions

Name: _____

# Daily Word Problems

## WEEK 34 • DAY 5

**School Fundraising**

Mr. Baker's class sold boxes of cookies to raise money for the Math Club. The following list shows the number of boxes that each club member sold in the first week:

8, 15, 17, 20, 12, 15, 5, 14, 20, 18, 10

1. Use the information to draw a box plot of the data.

**Boxes of Cookies Sold**

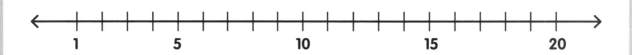

2. Find the following measures of variation for the data set.

median _____

range _____

first quartile _____

third quartile _____

interquartile range _____

3. Compare the lengths of the lines that extend to the left and right of the box. What do they tell you about the sales?

_____

_____

Name: _____

## Daily Word Problems

**WEEK 35 • DAY 1**

**On the Go**

Mike is a truck driver. One day he drove 220 miles in 4 hours. He still had 165 more miles to go.

How much more time did he need to complete his route if he continued driving the same speed?

Work Space:

Answer:

_____

---

Name: _____

## Daily Word Problems

**WEEK 35 • DAY 2**

**On the Go**

Carter was flying to Vancouver, Canada. Near the end of the trip, the pilot announced that the plane was 200 kilometers from the city. Carter wondered how many miles that was. The passenger next to him said that 1 kilometer is about 0.6 mile.

How many miles equals 200 kilometers?

Work Space:

Answer:

_____ miles

# Daily Word Problems

**WEEK 35 • DAY 3**

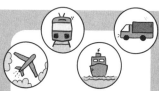

**On the Go**

Work Space:

The Water Bridge Ferry can carry either 15 cars or 12 trucks across the river. It never carries both cars and trucks on the same trip.

Yesterday, the ferry made 5 trips. Each trip carried a full load. The ferry carried a total of 69 cars and trucks. How many cars and how many trucks did it transport?

Answer:

_____ cars, _____ trucks

---

# Daily Word Problems

**WEEK 35 • DAY 4**

**On the Go**

Work Space:

Amira got on the underground subway at Station A. The station had an elevation of –15 feet. The deepest point in the tunnel had an elevation of –130 feet.

How much lower was Amira's elevation when she reached the deepest part of the tunnel?

Answer:

_____ feet lower

# Daily Word Problems
## WEEK 35 • DAY 5

**On the Go**

The Gilreath family is spending a week at Camp Serenity.
Use the map and key to answer the questions.

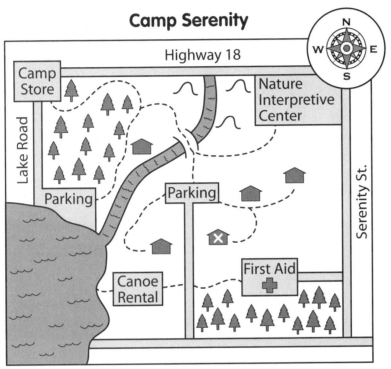

**Camp Serenity**

Highway 18

Camp Store

Nature Interpretive Center

Lake Road

Parking

Parking

First Aid

Canoe Rental

Serenity St.

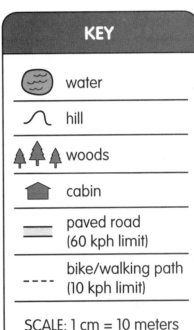

| KEY | |
|---|---|
| | water |
| | hill |
| | woods |
| | cabin |
| | paved road (60 kph limit) |
| --- | bike/walking path (10 kph limit) |

SCALE: 1 cm = 10 meters

1. Fiona is standing outside the family's cabin (with the **X**) and facing south.

   Which camp service is to her left? _____

   Which camp service is to her right? _____

2. Mr. Gilreath is going to the camp store to buy food for a hike. He can
   either ride his bike on the bike path or drive his car on the main roads.

   Which of Mr. Gilreath's options is the shorter distance? _____

   Which option would take Mr. Gilreath less time? _____

Name: _____

# Daily Word Problems

## WEEK 36 • DAY 1

**Batter Up!**

The bases (first base, second base, third base, home plate) on a baseball diamond are 90 feet apart. If the bases are "loaded," it means there is a player on first, second, and third base. If a batter hits a home run when the bases are loaded, it is a "grand slam." With a grand slam, four runs are scored by one home run!

What is the total number of feet that the four players run during a grand slam?

Work Space:

Answer:

_____ feet

---

Name: _____

# Daily Word Problems

## WEEK 36 • DAY 2

**Batter Up!**

A "batting average" is between .000 and 1.000. The higher the average, the better the player. To get this number, divide the number of hits (the times a player hit the ball and reached a base) by the total "at-bats" (the times a player went up to bat).

A player with 50 hits and 200 at-bats has a batting average of .250. How many hits would have given that player a batting average of .300?

Work Space:

Answer:

_____ hits

Name: _____

# Daily Word Problems

**WEEK 36 • DAY 3**

**Batter Up!**

The Missouri Middlers play 162 games every year. In the last 5 years, they have had a total of 410 wins and 400 losses.

1. What is the ratio of wins to losses in simplest terms?

2. If this ratio stays the same, how many wins and losses will the Missouri Middlers have in the upcoming year?

Work Space:

Answer:

1. _____

2. _____ wins, _____ losses

---

Name: _____

# Daily Word Problems

**WEEK 36 • DAY 4**

**Batter Up!**

Pitchers calculate their "earned run average," or ERA, to show how often a pitcher allows a batter on the opposite team to score a run in a 9-inning game. The lower the ERA, the better the pitcher. To get this number, divide the number of runs that the other team scored by the number of innings the pitcher pitched. Then multiply this quotient by 9.

If Joy pitched 8 innings during which 2 runs were scored, what is Joy's ERA?

Work Space:

Answer:

_____

# Daily Word Problems

## WEEK 36 • DAY 5

**Batter Up!**

The table lists the batting averages of five players.

| Player's Name | Batting Average |
|---|---|
| Kei | .250 |
| Antonio | .225 |
| Tracey | .200 |
| Dana | .175 |
| Rodrigo | .275 |

1. Suppose each of the players had a total of 80 at-bats. How many hits did each player have? (Hint: The batting averages are calculated by dividing the number of hits by the number of at-bats.)

   Kei _____ hits

   Antonio _____ hits

   Tracey _____ hits

   Dana _____ hits

   Rodrigo _____ hits

2. What is the mean batting average for this group of players?

   _____

# Answer Key

## Week 1

Day 1: 9 adults

Day 2: 3 paintings; 12th place, 24th place, and 36th place

Day 3: 1. 150 inches
2. 12 ½ feet

Day 4: 18 circles, 9 squares

Day 5: 1. 6,800 yd²
2. 400 yd
3. 850 yd²

## Week 2

Day 1: 1. 42 beads
2. 24 beads left over

Day 2: 2,700 dots

Day 3: 10 cups

Day 4: 0.05 m, 5 cm

Day 5: 1. 10 cm
2. 40 cm
3. 100 cm²
4. black – 1/5 OR 5/25, gray – 8/25, white – 12/25

## Week 3

Day 1: 1,460 dreams

Day 2: 1. 730 hours
2. 30 days

Day 3: 245 people would dream in color; 105 people would dream in black and white.

Day 4: 210 miles

Day 5: 1. 48 teaspoons
2. 3,072 calories
3. 2,560 grams

## Week 4

Day 1: 1 ⅞ cups

Day 2: 5 sticks, 1¼ pounds

Day 3: 1. 15,000 muffins per year
2. 50 muffins per day

Day 4: 240 customers

Day 5: Elise – cherry
Reshma – peach
Shondra – lemon
Jaime – apple
Winston – chocolate

## Week 5

Day 1: 700 beads

Day 2: $18.00

Day 3: Keiko got the better deal. Each of her books cost $1.25, and each of Bryan's books cost $1.45.

Day 4: 12 games

Day 5: 1. $1–$5
2. 70 items
3. 50 more
4. $21–$25
Possible answers: There weren't many items in this category. People didn't want to spend so much.

## Week 6

Day 1: 1. 276 stamps
2. 621 stamps combined

Day 2: 1. 480 in.³
2. Any 3 dimensions that multiply to 480; Example: 16 inches × 10 inches × 3 inches

Day 3: 1. $1.50
2. $15.00

Day 4: 40 stamps

Day 5: 1. Line graph should be completed as shown:

**Price of First-Class Stamps**

2. $9.80
3. $1.20
4. Any price from $0.55 to $0.60. Example: The price seems to go up a few cents every few years.

## Week 7

Day 1: Coupon A; 10 cans will cost $4.35. With Coupon B, 10 cans will cost $4.64.

Day 2: Cat's Meow; Its food costs $0.18 per ounce. Kitty Cuisine's food costs $0.19 per ounce.

Day 3: 1. 4/5
2. 12 dogs

Day 4: dogs – 32%, cats – 40%, hamsters – 28%

Day 5: 1. $1,900
2. $900
3. $425

## Week 8

Day 1: 1. 1/20
2. 0.05
3. 5%

Day 2: tax: $1.80
total cost: $21.80

Day 3: about 14¢

Day 4: 19,120 toasters

Day 5: 1. 12 ¾ in.
2. 12 in.
3. by ¾ in.
4. $\frac{315}{32}$ OR 9 $\frac{27}{32}$ in.²
5. $\frac{35}{4}$ OR 8 ¾ in.²
6. by 1 $\frac{3}{32}$ in.²

## Week 9

Day 1: $6.50

Day 2: student – 27 jelly beans
teacher – 17 jelly beans

Day 3: 8 inches long by 6 inches wide

Day 4: 24 photos

Day 5: 1. 8 balloons per package
2. 47 minutes, 20 seconds

## Week 10

Day 1: 30°C

Day 2: 6 days

Day 3: 20 cm

Day 4: 32.5 cm

Day 5: 1. 3 days
2. 15 days
3. 9 days

## Week 11

Day 1:  47 boxes

Day 2:  531 ounces

Day 3:  vegetables: 180 cans
        fruit: 120 cans

Day 4:  443 food items

Day 5:  1. 9 cans
        2. 27 cans
        3. 54 cans

## Week 12

Day 1:  1 hour, 38 minutes,
        14.71 seconds

Day 2:  528 miles

Day 3:  about 3 times faster

Day 4:  Danica, 4 minutes

Day 5:  Points: **A**–18, **B**–13, **C**–8,
        **D**–2, **E**–1

        The only drivers who can
        win must be able to beat
        the leader's 18 points in
        2 more races. **D** and **E**
        couldn't earn 18 points
        even if they won both
        races. **A**, **B**, or **C** could
        win because their current
        point totals are closer.

## Week 13

Day 1:  27 students

Day 2:  $129.60

Day 3:  3/8 of the total distance

Day 4:  1. January
        2. December
        3. February
        4. November
        5. March
        6. April

Day 5:  1. (65 × 4) + (170 × 2)
        2. $600
        3. $1,800

## Week 14

Day 1:  1. $6.60
        2. $1.65

Day 2:  3.5 hot dogs per minute,
        $78.40

Day 3:  25 packages of hot dogs,
        20 packages of buns

Day 4:  $3.45

Day 5:  1. 720
        2. 144
        3. 180 hot dogs; That mean
           makes the total sales
           900. 900 – 720 = 180.

## Week 15

Day 1:  average players: about 37%
        best players: about 47%

Day 2:  1.25 times faster

Day 3:  90%

Day 4:  253 ft$^2$

Day 5:  1. It will still be lower than
           Annie's. Skyler's will be
           +2, but Annie's is +5.
        2. Answers will vary.
           Example: Evgeny's team
           scored 4 goals, and the
           other team scored none.
           His team scored
           5 goals, and the other
           team scored 1 goal.

## Week 16

Day 1:  $1.32

Day 2:  Example: 65,000 steps.
        I rounded 12,543 to
        13,000. Then I multiplied
        13,000 by 5 to get 65,000.

Day 3:  5:56 p.m.

Day 4:  $29.25

Day 5:  1. (–3, 4)
        2. (–3, –3)
        3. (2, 4), 5 blocks
        4. (2, –3)

        Point should be added on
        the map as shown:

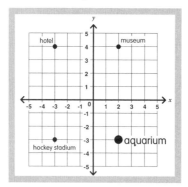

## Week 17

Day 1:  largest perimeter: 74 m
        dimensions: 1 m × 36 m

        smallest perimeter: 24 m
        dimensions: 6 m × 6 m

Day 2:  95 ft$^2$

Day 3:  1. 9 ft × 7 ft × 2 ft
        2. 84 ft$^3$ of soil

Day 4:  1. perimeter: 12 ft
           area: 6 ft$^2$
        2. new perimeter: 24 ft
           new area: 24 ft$^2$

Day 5:  The record sheet should
        be filled in as follows:

| Item | Income | Expense |
|---|---|---|
| Sales: plants | **7,380** | |
| Sales: tools/supplies | 6,035 | |
| Rent | | **–2,500** |
| Advertising | | **–400** |
| Purchase of new plants | | –3,200 |
| Utilities (water, electricity) | | –300 |
| Employee wages | | –4,000 |
| **Total** | **13,415** | **–10,400** |

        1. $13,415
        2. $10,400
        3. $3,015

## Week 18

Day 1:  Yes. The peak would be
        7,035 ft below sea level.

Day 2:  342,500 times longer

Day 3:  1. about 1,185 centimeters
        2. about 467 inches

Day 4:  295°F

Day 5:  1. 150$d$
           The glacier travels
           150 feet per day, so
           multiply the number
           of days by 150.
        2. 54,750 feet
        3. about 10 miles

## Week 19

Day 1:  3.75 more miles

Day 2:  15 miles per day

Day 3:  1. 2$r$
        2. 2$r$ = 270, 135 racers

Day 4:  2:27 p.m.

Day 5:  1. 135 racers
        2. 95 racers
        3. The data are clustered
           on the left side. More
           racers were younger.
           There were fewer racers
           as the ages went up.

## Week 20

Day 1:  650 square feet

Day 2:  30 cups

Day 3:  54, 72, 90

Day 4:  45 people

Day 5:  1. 80 bottles
        2. 1.2 cups
        3. 384 servings

## Week 21

Day 1: 1.5 Yumm dollars

Day 2: 1. 20 tacos
2. $2.50t \leq 25$, 10 tacos

Day 3: $78

Day 4: 240 in.$^2$

Day 5: 1. **F**–quadrant II
**W**–quadrant I
**S**–quadrant III
**Z**–quadrant IV

Points should be added on the grid as shown:

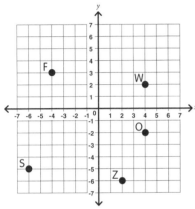

2. (4, −2), quadrant IV

## Week 22

Day 1: 28 in.$^2$

Day 2: 240 cm$^2$

Day 3: red−3, yellow−6, blue−9

Day 4: $f + 8 \geq 20$, 12 more flags

Day 5: 1. Triangle with area of 24 square units should be drawn. Example: base 12 in., height 4 in.
2. Rectangle with area of 18 square inches should be drawn. Example: base 9 in., height 2 in.

## Week 23

Day 1: $136

Day 2: $8

Day 3: $80

Day 4: 1. $35g$
2. $35g \leq 210$
6 grooming visits

---

Day 5: Map should be completed as shown:

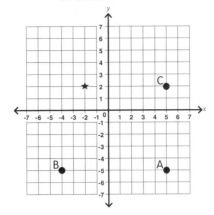

1. 9 blocks
2. 7 blocks
3. (−2, 2)
4. Canine Clips, 7 blocks

## Week 24

Day 1: volume: 45 ft$^3$
surface area: 87 ft$^2$

Day 2: 1. $1.25w$: the cost of the water, $1.75a$: the cost of the apple juice
2. $1.25(3) + 1.75(2)$, Total cost: $7.25

Day 3: $16s \leq 80$, maximum number of T-shirts: 5

Day 4: 180 miles

Day 5: 1. 5,600 cupcakes
2. $18,200
3. $312,000

## Week 25

Day 1: Examples:
base: 12 centimeters, height: 8 centimeters
OR base: 6 centimeters, height: 16 centimeters

Day 2: 7.5 OR 7 ½ inches

Day 3: 6 farm animals, 9 forest animals

Day 4: 10 cm$^2$

Day 5: 1. **A**−24 in.$^2$, **B**−40 in.$^2$, **C**−30 in.$^2$
2. 1,880 in.$^2$
3. 2 bottles

---

## Week 26

Day 1: $663

Day 2: 1. 25 years old
2. 26 years old

Day 3: 1. 36 students
2. $63

Day 4: 181 ft

Day 5: 1. 16,500 m$^2$
2. Lion Country is greater by 11,150 square meters.

## Week 27

Day 1: 15 people

Day 2: 1. Ramon
2. Cheri
3. The middle score is closest to the highest score (2 points away). It is 5 points away from the lowest score.

Day 3: 132 in.$^2$

Day 4: 469 points

Day 5: 1. 48 people
2. board games, 96 people
3. 24 more people
4. They would match.

## Week 28

Day 1: perimeter: 18 units
area: 12 square units

Day 2: Quadrilateral should be drawn as shown:

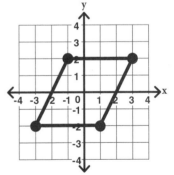

1. rhombus
2. 16 square units

Day 3: 46 cm$^2$
Explanations will vary. Example: I found each square's area (5 × 5 = 25). Together the area is 50 cm$^2$. The overlapping part is 4 cm$^2$ (2 × 2 = 4). Since that part is covered up on one square, I subtracted 4 from the total area.

Day 4:

4 lines of symmetry

Day 5:   16 tiles

## Week 29

Day 1:   41 pounds (22 + 19 pounds)

Day 2:   $82 + 61 + 39 + w \le 500$,
318 additional kg

Day 3:   1. 3/4 full
2. 9/16 full

Day 4:   2,016 meters

Day 5:   1. Plot should be
completed as shown:

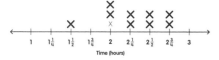

2. mean – 2¼,
median – 2¼, mode – 2
3. The median and mode
wouldn't be affected.
The mean would
increase slightly to
2⅓ hours.

## Week 30

Day 1:   paintings 23, 29, 31, 37,
41, 43, 47;
The numbers of the
paintings they stole were
prime numbers.

Day 2:   Ana: at the tree
Bob: on the bench
Cil: high up in the
building

Day 3:   the year 2029

Day 4:   calendar – $10
gardener – $20
Ms. Taban – $40

Day 5:   golden egg – Bugsy
glass slipper – Curly
enchanted mirror – Shifty
jeweled crown – Sneakers
magic bean seeds – Zappo

## Week 31

Day 1:   5 lb 6 oz

Day 2:   29 inches

Day 3:   volume: 2,880 cm³
surface area: 1,248 cm²

Day 4:   21 catfish, 35 trout

Day 5:   1. 45
2. 30
3. first quartile – 40
third quartile – 55
4. 15
5. Example: There is
a cluster of people
between 40 and 45
who like to fish. In the
third quartile, the ages
are more spread out.

## Week 32

Day 1:   The evening showing is
the better buy. With the
coupon, a ticket will cost
$12.00.

Day 2:   9 hours

Day 3:   1. 220 empty seats
2. 46%

Day 4:   295 people

Day 5:   1. median – 131
range – 32
first quartile – 118
third quartile – 140
interquartile range – 22
2. 130 minutes

## Week 33

Day 1:   4 ft²

Day 2:   Closet A: 180 shoes
Closet B: 60 shoes
Each closet: 120 shoes

Day 3:   beagle; The beagle took
3 minutes to bury 1 bone,
and the basset hound
took 4 minutes.

Day 4:   Crystal – 27 sweaters
Flake – 36 sweaters

Day 5:   1. 9 ft long, 7 ft wide
2. 63 ft²
3. 48 ft²
4. 15 ft²
Example: I subtracted the
garden's area (48 ft²) from
the total area (63 ft²).

## Week 34

Day 1:   $12.50 + p \le 50.00$,
$37.50

Day 2:   $700 more

Day 3:   105 cards

Day 4:   58 subscriptions

Day 5:   1. Box plot should be
completed as shown:

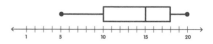

2. median – 15
range – 15
first quartile – 10
third quartile – 18
interquartile range – 8
3. The line on the right is
shorter than the line on
the left. This means the
sales in the top quarter
had less variation than
the sales in the bottom
quarter.

## Week 35

Day 1:   3 more hours

Day 2:   120 miles

Day 3:   45 cars, 24 trucks

Day 4:   115 feet lower

Day 5:   1. First Aid, Canoe Rental
2. the bike path, the road

## Week 36

Day 1:   900 feet

Day 2:   60 hits

Day 3:   1. 41:40
2. 82 wins, 80 losses

Day 4:   2.25

Day 5:   1. Kei – 20 hits
Antonio – 18 hits
Tracey – 16 hits
Dana – 14 hits
Rodrigo – 22 hits
2. .225

Daily Word Problems • EMC 3096 • © Evan-Moor Corp.

# Day-by-Day Skills List

## Week 1

| Day | Skills |
| --- | --- |
| 1 | Division; Ratios and rates |
| 2 | Factors and multiples |
| 3 | Division; Fractions; Linear measurement |
| 4 | Ratios and rates |
| 5 | Division; Fractions; Perimeter and area |

## Week 2

| Day | Skills |
| --- | --- |
| 1 | Division |
| 2 | Addition and subtraction; Multiplication |
| 3 | Ratios and rates |
| 4 | Multiplication; Division; Decimals; Linear measurement |
| 5 | Fractions; Perimeter and area |

## Week 3

| Day | Skills |
| --- | --- |
| 1 | Multiplication |
| 2 | Multiplication; Division; Time and temperature |
| 3 | Fractions |
| 4 | Fractions; Time and temperature; Linear measurement |
| 5 | Multiplication; Weight and capacity |

## Week 4

| Day | Skills |
| --- | --- |
| 1 | Fractions; Weight and capacity |
| 2 | Multiplication; Division; Fractions; Weight and capacity |
| 3 | Multiplication; Division |
| 4 | Fractions; Ratios and rates |
| 5 | Logical thinking |

## Week 5

| Day | Skills |
| --- | --- |
| 1 | Addition and subtraction |
| 2 | Addition and subtraction; Multiplication; Decimals |
| 3 | Division; Decimals; Ratios and rates |
| 4 | Fractions |
| 5 | Addition and subtraction; Graphs, charts, and maps |

## Week 6

| Day | Skills |
| --- | --- |
| 1 | Addition and subtraction; Multiplication; Division; Fractions |
| 2 | Surface area and volume |
| 3 | Multiplication; Decimals |
| 4 | Logical thinking |
| 5 | Addition and subtraction; Multiplication; Decimals; Graphs, charts, and maps |

## Week 7

| Day | Skills |
|-----|--------|
| 1 | Addition and subtraction; Multiplication; Division; Decimals; Percents |
| 2 | Decimals; Ratios and rates |
| 3 | Fractions; Ratios and rates |
| 4 | Division; Percents |
| 5 | Addition and subtraction; Division; Graphs, charts, and maps |

## Week 8

| Day | Skills |
|-----|--------|
| 1 | Fractions; Decimals; Percents |
| 2 | Addition and subtraction; Multiplication; Percents |
| 3 | Division; Decimals; Ratios and rates |
| 4 | Division |
| 5 | Addition and subtraction; Fractions; Perimeter and area |

## Week 9

| Day | Skills |
|-----|--------|
| 1 | Division; Decimals |
| 2 | Addition and subtraction; Multiplication; Division |
| 3 | Perimeter and area |
| 4 | Multiplication; Percents |
| 5 | Multiplication; Factors and multiples; Time and temperature |

## Week 10

| Day | Skills |
|-----|--------|
| 1 | Positive and negative numbers; Addition and subtraction |
| 2 | Multiplication; Percents |
| 3 | Multiplication; Decimals; Linear measurement |
| 4 | Addition and subtraction; Decimals; Linear measurement |
| 5 | Addition and subtraction; Multiplication; Percents; Graphs, charts, and maps |

## Week 11

| Day | Skills |
|-----|--------|
| 1 | Division |
| 2 | Multiplication; Decimals |
| 3 | Multiplication; Ratios and rates |
| 4 | Positive and negative numbers; Addition and subtraction |
| 5 | Multiplication; Division; Linear measurement; Spatial reasoning |

## Week 12

| Day | Skills |
|-----|--------|
| 1 | Addition and subtraction; Decimals; Time and temperature |
| 2 | Addition and subtraction; Percents |
| 3 | Division; Ratios and rates |
| 4 | Addition and subtraction; Multiplication; Division; Time and temperature |
| 5 | Addition and subtraction; Logical thinking |

 Daily Word Problems • EMC 3096 • © Evan-Moor Corp.

## Week 13

| Day | Skills |
|-----|--------|
| 1 | Multiplication; Division; Fractions |
| 2 | Addition and subtraction; Multiplication; Percents |
| 3 | Addition and subtraction; Fractions |
| 4 | Positive and negative numbers; Time and temperature |
| 5 | Addition and subtraction; Multiplication; Fractions; Expressions and equations |

## Week 14

| Day | Skills |
|-----|--------|
| 1 | Addition and subtraction; Division; Decimals |
| 2 | Multiplication; Division; Decimals; Ratios and rates |
| 3 | Addition and subtraction; Percents |
| 4 | Addition and subtraction; Multiplication; Percents |
| 5 | Addition and subtraction; Division; Statistics; Graphs, charts, and maps |

## Week 15

| Day | Skills |
|-----|--------|
| 1 | Division; Percents |
| 2 | Division; Decimals |
| 3 | Division; Percents |
| 4 | Perimeter and area |
| 5 | Positive and negative numbers |

## Week 16

| Day | Skills |
|-----|--------|
| 1 | Decimals; Ratios and rates |
| 2 | Multiplication |
| 3 | Time and temperature |
| 4 | Multiplication; Division; Decimals; Ratios and rates; Logical thinking |
| 5 | Coordinate plane; Spatial reasoning |

## Week 17

| Day | Skills |
|-----|--------|
| 1 | Perimeter and area |
| 2 | Expressions and equations; Perimeter and area |
| 3 | Fractions; Surface area and volume; Spatial reasoning |
| 4 | Perimeter and area |
| 5 | Positive and negative numbers; Addition and subtraction; Graphs, charts, and maps |

## Week 18

| Day | Skills |
|-----|--------|
| 1 | Addition and subtraction |
| 2 | Division; Linear measurement |
| 3 | Division; Decimals; Linear measurement |
| 4 | Positive and negative numbers; Addition and subtraction; Time and temperature |
| 5 | Multiplication; Division; Expressions and equations; Linear measurement |

**Week 19**

| Day | Skills |
|-----|--------|
| 1 | Decimals; Ratios and rates; Time and temperature |
| 2 | Addition and subtraction; Division; Statistics |
| 3 | Division; Expressions and equations |
| 4 | Time and temperature |
| 5 | Addition and subtraction; Statistics; Graphs, charts, and maps |

**Week 20**

| Day | Skills |
|-----|--------|
| 1 | Perimeter and area; Spatial reasoning |
| 2 | Multiplication; Division; Fractions; Weight and capacity |
| 3 | Factors and multiples |
| 4 | Statistics |
| 5 | Multiplication; Division; Weight and capacity |

**Week 21**

| Day | Skills |
|-----|--------|
| 1 | Division; Ratios and rates |
| 2 | Division; Inequalities |
| 3 | Addition and subtraction; Multiplication; Percents |
| 4 | Surface area and volume |
| 5 | Coordinate plane |

**Week 22**

| Day | Skills |
|-----|--------|
| 1 | Perimeter and area; Spatial reasoning |
| 2 | Perimeter and area; Spatial reasoning |
| 3 | Ratios and rates |
| 4 | Addition and subtraction; Inequalities |
| 5 | Perimeter and area; Spatial reasoning |

**Week 23**

| Day | Skills |
|-----|--------|
| 1 | Division |
| 2 | Factors and multiples |
| 3 | Addition and subtraction; Multiplication; Percents |
| 4 | Division; Inequalities |
| 5 | Coordinate plane |

**Week 24**

| Day | Skills |
|-----|--------|
| 1 | Surface area and volume; Fractions |
| 2 | Addition and subtraction; Multiplication; Decimals; Expressions and equations |
| 3 | Division; Inequalities |
| 4 | Multiplication; Decimals; Expressions and equations |
| 5 | Multiplication; Decimals |

## Week 25

| Day | Skills |
| --- | --- |
| 1 | Perimeter and area |
| 2 | Fractions; Linear measurement |
| 3 | Ratios and rates |
| 4 | Perimeter and area |
| 5 | Multiplication; Division; Surface area and volume |

## Week 26

| Day | Skills |
| --- | --- |
| 1 | Addition and subtraction; Multiplication; Percents |
| 2 | Statistics |
| 3 | Multiplication; Fractions; Decimals |
| 4 | Positive and negative numbers |
| 5 | Perimeter and area |

## Week 27

| Day | Skills |
| --- | --- |
| 1 | Division |
| 2 | Positive and negative numbers |
| 3 | Surface area and volume |
| 4 | Division |
| 5 | Addition and subtraction; Multiplication; Percents; Graphs, charts, and maps |

## Week 28

| Day | Skills |
| --- | --- |
| 1 | Perimeter and area |
| 2 | Perimeter and area; Coordinate plane; Spatial reasoning |
| 3 | Perimeter and area; Spatial reasoning |
| 4 | Spatial reasoning |
| 5 | Spatial reasoning |

## Week 29

| Day | Skills |
| --- | --- |
| 1 | Addition and subtraction; Percents |
| 2 | Addition and subtraction; Inequalities |
| 3 | Addition and subtraction; Multiplication; Fractions |
| 4 | Positive and negative numbers |
| 5 | Statistics; Graphs, charts, and maps |

## Week 30

| Day | Skills |
| --- | --- |
| 1 | Factors and multiples |
| 2 | Spatial reasoning |
| 3 | Logical thinking |
| 4 | Multiplication; Fractions; Logical thinking |
| 5 | Logical thinking |

## Week 31

| Day | Skills |
|-----|--------|
| 1 | Weight and capacity |
| 2 | Fractions; Linear measurement |
| 3 | Surface area and volume |
| 4 | Ratios and rates |
| 5 | Statistics; Graphs, charts, and maps |

## Week 32

| Day | Skills |
|-----|--------|
| 1 | Percents |
| 2 | Time and temperature |
| 3 | Percents |
| 4 | Addition and subtraction; Multiplication; Statistics |
| 5 | Statistics |

## Week 33

| Day | Skills |
|-----|--------|
| 1 | Surface area and volume |
| 2 | Logical thinking |
| 3 | Ratios and rates |
| 4 | Fractions; Logical thinking |
| 5 | Addition and subtraction; Surface area and volume; Spatial reasoning |

## Week 34

| Day | Skills |
|-----|--------|
| 1 | Addition and subtraction; Inequalities |
| 2 | Addition and subtraction; Multiplication; Division; Fractions |
| 3 | Division |
| 4 | Ratios and rates |
| 5 | Statistics; Graphs, charts, and maps |

## Week 35

| Day | Skills |
|-----|--------|
| 1 | Ratios and rates |
| 2 | Multiplication; Decimals; Linear measurement |
| 3 | Factors and multiples; Logical thinking |
| 4 | Positive and negative numbers |
| 5 | Ratios and rates; Linear measurement; Graphs, charts, and maps; Spatial reasoning |

## Week 36

| Day | Skills |
|-----|--------|
| 1 | Addition and subtraction; Multiplication; Linear measurement; Spatial reasoning |
| 2 | Division; Decimals; Ratios and rates |
| 3 | Ratios and rates |
| 4 | Ratios and rates |
| 5 | Multiplication; Decimals; Statistics |